baking

NEW
HOLLAND

contents

Introduction

This delicious collection of breads, cakes, cookies, tea breads, tray bakes and more is sure to tempt your tastebuds and appeal to a wide audience. There are recipes here that are suitable to make for any occasion including everday eating with the family, catering for school fêtes, and making a stunning centrepiece that is perfect to serve at a special occasion.

Baking is booming in popularity, an activity fuelled in part by a whole raft of light-hearted television programmes that encourage us all to don our pinnies, whip out the cookware and get creative in the kitchen. In reality, it takes so little effort to make something delicious to eat. Baking is a win-win activity. Not only is there great pleasure to be had in the activity of beating, blending and processing cake batter, or kneading and rolling bread and cookie dough, but the results are sure to be appreciated by everyone. And while you wait for your items to bake, the sweet and fragrant aroma of cooking that emanates from the kitchen and wafts in the air is sure to tempt the tastebuds and whet the appetite.

Here is a fabulous assortment of recipes for traditional and savoury breads to serve alongside soups, salads and main courses; sweet and salty muffins; crunchy, chewy and melt-in-the-mouth cookies; a whole range of scones on to which you can lavish butter and preserves; as well as a tempting array of cakes, tea breads and tray bakes that can be dressed up or down depending upon the occasion. Pastry features too and there is a delightful selection of crowd-pleasing sweet and savoury confections that you can make using minimal ingredients. But before you begin there are a few instructions that you need to take note of to ensure that you get the best results for your efforts.

Bakeware

If you're starting out and just want to buy the basics, you'll find you actually need very little equipment for baking, though as your confidence and repertoire grow, so too will your desire to have a broader range of equipment. A food processor is one of the most expensive pieces of kit, though it's definitely not essential— sure it makes light work of kneading dough, or whipping up a batch of cookie dough, but you can do the job just as well by hand, using a mixing bowl and a wooden spoon. It may take a little longer, and require a little elbow grease, but many cooks prefer the good old-fashioned methods of baking, liking the feel of the batter as it is mixed and blended and knowing from experience when to beat a little more or when to add a more wet or dry ingredients to make the mix just right.

A mixing bowl is a basic requirement, but if you really are starting with nothing, you could cream cake batters and cookie doughs in a large pan (pot) instead. A wooden spoon is essential, and so is a spatula, some accurate kitchen scales and and handful of tins (pans) in which to bake your items.

With bakeware it usually follows that the more expensive the item, the better the quality you purchase. Cake tins, in particular, can make quite a difference to how an item turns out. Inexpensive tins are likely to buckle more easily, last for less time, or conduct the heat less efficiently than costly ones, so as you gain experience and learn which items you use the most you can replace the cheap items in your cupboards with better quality ones. To start with you're most likely to need a couple of baking sheets, a square or rectangular tray bake pan for brownies, a 9 in (23 cm) deep-sided round cake tin, and a muffin tray (patty pan). Always use the correct size of tin quoted in the recipe, otherwise your cake may not bake according to the instructions.

Test your oven regularly too. It's a good idea to buy an oven thermometer and adjust your oven temperature up or down to make sure you bake at the correct temperature. Conventional ovens are hotter at the top than the base so you should always positions cakes in the centre of the oven when you bake them. If you are baking two items, one above the other on two oven shelves then swap them over half way through the baking time to ensure that both bake evenly. Similarly if you are fitting two items side-by-side ensure that you swap the positions of each as well as turning each item around just in case your oven has hot spots and cooks unevenly. Make sure the oven shelves are level too.

Before you begin
Read the recipe through from start to finish and make sure you understand what to do at each stage of the recipe. Always allow sufficient time to make the goods. Once you start baking, you need to continue until the item is complete. If you break off in the middle, for instance, realising that you don't have the time to wait for the cake to bake once it is made, then the ingredients will be ruined, an expense and a waste that nobody wants.

Get all the equipment out of the cupboards that you will need and assemble them on a clean work surface. Similarly locate all of the ingredients and weigh them all out before you begin just to be doubly sure that you have them all to hand. When you weigh out the ingredients use metric, imperial or cup measurements and stick rigidly to your preferred choice. Never use a combination of the measurements because there is a slight difference in the conversions.

Note
A couple of the recipes use uncooked eggs in their creation. Never give foods containing uncooked eggs to sick or elderly people, pregnant women or young children.

yeast & snack breads

Jewish egg loaf

12 oz (350 g/3 cups)
  unbleached strong white
  bread flour, sifted, plus
  extra for dusting
1 teaspoon salt
2½ oz (65 g/⅓ cup) sugar
¼ oz (7 g) dry yeast
2 eggs, beaten, plus extra for
  glazing
2 tablespoons oil
¼ pint (150 ml/⅔ cup)
  hand-hot water
oil, for greasing
1 tablespoon poppy seeds, for
  coating

makes 1 loaf

In a large mixing bowl, mix together the flour, salt, sugar and yeast. Add the eggs, oil and water and mix together with your hand. Knead by hand in the bowl until the dough is very soft, silky and elastic. Cover with a kitchen towel and leave to rise in a warm place until doubled in size, about 1 hour.

Turn the dough out on to a lightly floured surface and knock back (punch down) the dough to release the air.

Divide the dough into three equal portions and on a lightly floured surface roll each into a rope. Make sure that they are all of equal length, and tapered at each end. Braid (plait) the ropes together and tuck the ends under. Arrange on a lightly greased baking sheet and cover with a cloth. Set aside until risen, about 1 hour.

Preheat the oven to 350°F/180°C/Gas mark 4.

Brush the bread with beaten egg and scatter with poppy seeds.

Bake for 40 minutes or until the bread sounds hollow when tapped on the underside. Turn out on to a wire rack to go cold.

Irish soda bread

5 oz (155 g/1⅓ cups) plain
(all-purpose) flour, plus
extra for dusting
1 teaspoon baking soda
1 teaspoon salt
1½ oz (45 g) butter, plus
extra for greasing
16 fl oz (475 ml/2 cups)
buttermilk or milk

makes 1 loaf

Preheat oven to 400°F/200°C/Gas mark 6.

Sift the flour, baking soda and salt into a mixing
bowl. Rub in the butter using your fingertips, until
the mixture resembles coarse breadcrumbs. Make
a well in the centre of the flour mixture, pour in the
milk or buttermilk and, using a round-ended knife,
mix to form a soft dough.

Turn the dough out onto a floured surface and
knead lightly until smooth. Shape into a 7 in (18 cm)
round, and place on a greased and floured baking
sheet. Score the loaf into eighths using a sharp
knife.

Dust lightly with flour and bake for 35–40 minutes,
or until the loaf sounds hollow when tapped on
the base.

Wholemeal bread

4 oz (115 g/1 cup)
    wholemeal (whole-wheat)
    self-raising (self-rising)
    flour
4 oz (115 g/1 cup) white
    self-raising (self-rising)
    flour
½ pint (300 ml/1¼ cups)
    skimmed milk
oil, for greasing
1 teaspoon dry mustard
    (powder)
1 tablespoon sesame seeds

makes 1 loaf

Preheat the oven to 400°F/200°C/Gas mark 6.

Sift the flour into a large bowl. Return the husks from the sieve to the bowl. Stir in enough skimmed milk to give a sticky dough. Knead on a lightly floured surface until smooth, shape into a round.

Place the dough on a greased baking sheet, press out with fingers to about 1 in (2.5 cm) thick. Using a sharp knife, mark into wedges, and cut the wedges into the dough about ½ in/12 mm deep.

Sprinkle the dough with mustard and sesame seeds. Bake for 30 minutes or until golden brown and the bread sounds hollow on the underside when tapped.

Pide

13½ oz (390 g/3⅓ cups)
  plain (all-purpose) flour
¼ oz (7 g) dry yeast
Pinch of salt
1 teaspoon sugar
2 tablespoons olive oil, plus
  extra for greasing
1 egg, lightly beaten
2 tablespoons sesame seeds

makes 2 loaves

Combine the flour, yeast, salt and sugar in a large bowl. Make a well in the centre. Stir in 12 fl oz (350 ml/1½ cups) warm water and the olive oil. Mix to make a soft dough.

Turn out onto a lightly floured surface and knead for 10 minutes, adding a little more flour or liquid, as needed, until soft, elastic and smooth. Place in a lightly oiled bowl. Turn to coat with oil. Cover with a kitchen towel and set aside in a warm place for 1 hour, or until doubled in size.

Turn the flour out onto a lightly floured surface. Knock back (punch down) the dough to remove the air. Divide into two equal portions and roll each into a ball. Put each on separate greased baking sheets, cover with clean kitchen towels and set aside to rise again in a warm place for 20–30 minutes.

Preheat the oven to 425°F/220°C/Gas mark 7.

Flatten each ball to make a 10 in (25 cm) circle. Pull into an oval shape. Make indentations over the surface with your fingertips, leaving a 1 in (2.5 cm) border. Brush generously with egg. Sprinkle with sesame seeds and bake for 15 minutes, or until golden. Set aside to go cold.

Israeli Ka'kat

1 lb (450 g/4 cups)
   unbleached strong white
   bread flour, plus extra for
   dusting
¼ oz (7 g) dry yeast
1 tablespoon sugar
1 teaspoon salt
oil, for greasing
1 egg white, mixed with
   1 teaspoon water
5 oz (150 g/1 cup) sesame
   seeds

makes 8

Mix the flour, yeast, salt, sugar together in a large bowl. Add 15 fl oz (425 ml/1 cup) hand hot water and mix to a soft dough.

Turn out onto a lightly floured work surface and knead until smooth, elastic and silky. Return the dough to an oiled bowl, cover with a kitchen towel and set aside in a warm place to rise until doubled in size, about 1 hour.

Knock back (punch down) the dough and divide into 8 equal pieces. Roll each into a long log and join the ends so that the join is invisible. Place the ropes on a greased baking sheet, twisting each to form knot. Space them about 2 in (5 cm) apart.

Brush the dough liberally with the egg white mixed with water and sprinkle generously with sesame seeds. Cover with a kitchen towel and leave to rise for 20 minutes.

Preheat the oven to 400°F/200°C/Gas mark 6. Bake the risen dough for 15–20 minutes until golden.

Baps

1 teaspoon sugar
1 tablespoon gelatine
¼ oz (7 g) dry yeast
2 egg whites
1 teaspoon salt
½ teaspoon citric acid
9 oz (250 g/2¼ cups) strong
  white bread flour, plus
  extra for dusting
2 tablespoons olive oil, plus
  extra for greasing

makes 12

Pour 7 fl oz (200 ml) of cold water into a glass bowl. Add the sugar and gelatine and set aside for 1 minute to soften. Heat the gelatine mixture in the microwave for 50 seconds. Add the yeast and set aside for 10 minutes.

Whisk the egg whites, salt and citric acid in a separate bowl until stiff using an electric beater. Tip the flour into the yeast mixture. Beat in the oil and whisked eggs for 1 minute with an electric beater Cover and let stand again for 10 minutes.

Preheat the oven to 350°F/180°C/Gas mark 4. Grease a 12-cup jumbo muffin tray.

Spoon the mixture into the cups of the muffin tray and leave until puffy, about 15 minutes.

Dust the tops with sifted flour. Bake for 10 minutes. Remove from the oven and wrap in a clean kitchen towel until cold.

Naan bread

8 oz (225 g/1 cup) natural
(plain) yogurt
8 oz (225 g/2 cups) plain
(all-purpose) flour
12 oz (350 g/3 cups)
wholemeal (whole-wheat)
plain (all-purpose) flour
1 tablespoon yeast
2 teaspoons salt
1 teaspoon sugar
2 tablespoon nut oil, plus
extra for greasing
3 tablespoon black sesame
seeds
4 oz (115 g/ ½ cup) sesame
seeds

makes 8

Preheat the oven to 230°C/450°F/Gas mark 8. Lightly grease two baking sheets.

In a bowl, mix the yogurt with 12 fl oz (350 ml/ ½ cups) boiling water and stir well. Set aside for 5 minutes. In another bowl, mix the plain flour with 4 oz (115 g/1 cup) of the wholemeal flour and add the yeast. Add the yogurt mixture and stir with a wooden spoon for 3 minutes, then cover with cling film (plastic wrap). Allow to rest for 1 hour.

Add the salt, sugar, oil and black sesame seeds and enough of the remaining flour to form a firm but moist dough. Begin to knead on a floured surface and continue until the dough is very silky and elastic. Allow the dough to rise in an oiled bowl for 1 hour at room temperature, or until doubled in size.

Knock back (punch down) the dough and divide into 8 pieces. Shape each into a ball then flatten each into a rough circle about ½ in (12 mm) thick. Transfer to the prepared baking sheets.

Brush the surface of the dough with water and sprinkle generously with sesame seeds. Cover and allow to rise for 10 minutes. Bake for 5–8 minutes.

Hot cross buns

¾ oz/21 g) dried yeast
8 fl oz (250 ml/1 cup)
  lukewarm milk
Pinch of salt
2 tablespoons sugar
1 teaspoon ground cinnamon
  (powder)
½ teaspoon ground nutmeg
  (powder)
¼ teaspoon mixed (apple pie)
  spice
2 eggs
1 lb (450 g/4 cups) plain (all-
  purpose) flour, plus extra
  for dusting
2 tablespoons oil, plus extra
  for greasing
4 oz (115 g) dried fruit

CROSS & GLAZE
2 oz (55 g/½ cup) plain
  (all-purpose) flour
2 tablespoons milk
2 tablespoons icing
  (confectioners') sugar

makes 18

Put the yeast in a large bowl. Pour in the milk and set aside in warm place for 10 minutes, or until frothy. Stir in the salt, sugar and spices. Beat in the eggs, one at a time. Stir in half the flour to make a soft dough. Beat in the oil and continue beating for 1 minute. Knead in the remaining flour. Place the dough in a clean, lightly oiled bowl. Turn to coat with oil. Cover with a kitchen towel and set aside in a warm place for 1 hour, or until doubled in size.

Knead the dough, working in the dried fruit on a lightly floured surface. Roll into a log. Cut into 18 even pieces. Shape into rounds and place 1 in (2.5 cm) apart, on greased baking sheets. Cover and set aside to rise in a warm place for 20 minutes.

Preheat the oven to 400°F/200°C/Gas mark 6. To make the cross, put the flour and 2½ fl oz (75 ml/ ⅓ cup) water in a bowl. Beat until smooth. Spoon into a piping bag fitted with a plain nozzle. Pipe a cross on top of each bun.

Bake for 15 minutes or until golden.

For the glaze, warm the milk and mix with the icing sugar in a bowl. Mix until smooth. Brush the glaze over the buns.

Apple loaves

8 oz (225 g/2 cups)
  all-purpose (plain) flour,
  plus extra for dusting
1¾ oz (45 g/¼ cup)
  granulated (white) sugar,
  plus extra for dusting
2 teaspoons baking powder
½ teaspoon bicarbonate of
  soda (baking soda)
½ teaspoon salt
1½ oz (40 g) butter, chilled,
  plus extra for greasing
1 cooking apple, peeled and
  grated (shredded)
4 fl oz (120 ml/½ cup) milk,
  plus extra for glazing
ground cinnamon (powder),
  for dusting

makes 2 loaves

Preheat the oven to 425°F/220°C/Gas mark 7.
Grease two baking sheets.

Combine the flour, sugar, baking powder,
bicarbonate of soda and salt in a large bowl. Cut in
the butter until crumbly.

Add the apple and milk. Stir to form a soft dough.
Turn out onto a lightly floured surface. Knead gently
8–10 times. Divide into two and pat into even
rounds.

Place on the prepared baking sheets. Brush the tops
with milk. Sprinkle with sugar, then with cinnamon.

Score each top into six pie-shaped wedges. Bake
for 15 minutes until browned and risen. Serve warm
with butter.

Country cornbread

4 oz (115 g/1 cup) cornmeal
  (polenta)
4 oz (115 g/1 cup) plain
  (all-purpose) flour
2 tablespoons sugar
1 tablespoon baking powder
½ teaspoon salt
6 fl oz (175 ml/¾ cup) milk
4 fl oz (120 ml/½ cup) sour
  cream
2 eggs
3½ oz (100 g) butter, melted,
  plus extra for greasing

makes 1 loaf

Preheat the oven to 350°F/180°C/Gas mark 4.
Grease and line a 9 in (23 cm)square cake tin (pan).

Sift all the dry ingredients together into a large
bowl.

In another bowl, beat the melted butter, milk, cream
and eggs until blended. Mix with the flour mixture
until just combined.

Pour the batter into the prepared tin. Bake for
approximately 30 minutes, or until a skewer inserted
into the centre comes out clean. Cut into squares or
rectangles and serve warm.

Basil beer bread

oil, *for greasing*
8 oz (225 g/2 cups)
  self-raising (self-rising)
  flour, sifted
2 oz (55 g) sugar
¾ *cup fresh basil, chopped*
1 *teaspoon crushed black*
  peppercorns
8 fl oz (250 ml/1 cup) beer,
  at room temperature

makes 1 loaf

Preheat the oven to 350°F/180°C/Gas mark 4.
Grease and line a 4 x 8 in/11 x 21 cm loaf tin (pan).

Put the flour, sugar, basil, peppercorns and beer in a
bowl and mix to make a soft dough.

Arrange the dough in the prepared tin (pan) and
bake for 50 minutes, or until bread is cooked and a
skewer, when inserted into the centre, comes
out clean

Leave to set in the tin for 5 minutes before turning
out onto a wire rack to cool. Serve warm or cold
spread with olive or sun-dried tomato paste.

Herbed beer bread

8 oz (225 g/2 cups) plain
(all-purpose) flour
1 teaspoon baking soda
1½ oz (45 g) Parmesan,
grated (shredded)
2 tablespoons pitted black
olives, chopped
2 tablespoons olive oil
6 fl oz (175 ml/¾ cup) beer
¾ cup mixed fresh herbs,
chopped, for example,
parsley, basil, coriander
(cilantro) and oregano
milk, for glazing

makes 1 loaf

Preheat the oven to 350°F/180°C/Gas mark 4.
Grease and line a 3 x 8 in/8 x 20 cm loaf tin (pan).

Combine the flour, baking soda, Parmesan and
olives in a bowl. Make a well in the centre. Mix in the
oil and enough beer to make a moist dough.

Spoon one-third of the dough into the prepared tin.
Scatter over half of the herbs. Top with one-third of
the remaining dough. Scatter with the remaining
herbs. Top with the remaining dough. Brush with a
little milk.

Bake for 1 hour, or until the base sounds hollow
when tapped.

easy bakes

Traditional scones

8 oz (225 g/2 cups)
  self-rising (self-raising)
  flour, plus extra for
  dusting
1 teaspoon baking powder
2 teaspoons sugar
1½ oz (40 g) butter, cold,
  plus extra for greasing
1 egg
4 fl oz (120 ml/½ cup) milk
butter and preserve, to serve

makes 12

Preheat the oven to 425°F/220°C/Gas mark 7.
Grease and dust a baking sheet with flour.

Sift together the flour and baking powder into a
large bowl. Stir in the sugar, then rub in the butter
using your fingertips, until the mixture resembles
coarse breadcrumbs.

In a small bowl, whisk together the egg and milk.
Make a well in the centre of the flour mixture, pour
in the egg mixture and mix to form a soft dough.
Turn onto a lightly floured surface and knead lightly.

Roll out the dough to a ¾ in (2 cm) thickness. Stamp
out scones using a floured 2 in (5 cm) cookie cutter.

Arrange on the prepared baking sheet allowing
room for each to expand when baking. Brush
with a little milk then bake for 12–15 minutes, or
until golden. Serve with butter and your favourite
preserve.

Wholemeal scones

4 oz (115 g/1 cup)
  wholemeal (whole-wheat)
  self-raising (self-rising)
  flour
4 oz (115 g/1 cup)
  self-raising (self-rising)
  flour
2¼ oz (60 g/1 cup)
  unprocessed wheat bran
1 oz (30 g) sugar
2 oz (55 g) butter, cold, plus
  extra for greasing
8 fl oz (250 ml/1 cup) milk
butter, to serve

makes about 15

Preheat the oven to 350°F/180°C/Gas mark 4.
Grease and dust a baking sheet with flour.

Sift the flours into a bowl, return the husks from
the sieve to the bowl and mix in the bran. Add the
sugar. Rub in the butter until the mixture resembles
coarse breadcrumbs.

Make a well in the centre of the dry ingredients, stir
in enough milk to give a soft, sticky dough.

Turn the dough out onto a lightly floured surface
and knead lightly until smooth. Roll out to a
thickness of ¾ in (2 cm) and stamp outrounds using
a 2 in (5 cm) cookie cutter.

Arrange on the baking sheet. Bake for 15 minutes,
or until golden brown.

Date scones

1 lb (450 g/4 cups)
    self-raising (self-rising)
    flour, plus extra for
    dusting
1 teaspoon salt
2 teaspoons ground
    cinnamon (powder)
2 oz (55 g) butter, cold, plus
    extra for greasing
4 oz (115 g) dates, chopped
1 oz (30 g) sugar
16 fl oz (475 ml/2 cups) milk
1 egg beaten with 2 fl oz
    (50 ml/¼ cup) milk,
    to glaze
butter to serve,

makes 12–16

Preheat the oven to 450°F/230°C/Gas mark 8.
Grease and dust a baking sheet with flour.

Sift the flour, salt and cinnamon into a large bowl.
Add the butter and rub in using your fingertips, until
the mixture resembles coarse breadcrumbs. Add
the dates and the sugar. Make a well in the centre
and add the milk all at once, stirring quickly and
lightly to form a soft dough.

Turn onto a lightly floured surface and knead just
enough to make a smooth surface and roll out to
¾ in (2 cm) thick. Stamp out rounds using a 2 in
(5 cm) cookie cutter.

Arrange on the baking sheet. Brush the tops with
the combined beaten egg and milk and then bake
for about 10 minutes, or until golden.

Cheese scones

1 lb (450 g/4 cups)
   self-raising (self-rising)
   flour, plus extra for
   dusting
¼ teaspoon cayenne pepper
1 teaspoon salt
2 oz (55 g) butter, plus extra
   for greasing
1 tablespoon finely chopped
   onion
2 oz (55 g) Cheddar cheese,
   grated (shredded)
1 egg
¼ cup parsley, finely chopped
16 fl oz (475 ml/2 cups) milk
1 egg beaten with 2 fl oz
   (50 ml/¼ cup) milk,
   to glaze
butter, to serve

makes 12–16

Preheat the oven to 450°F/230°C/Gas mark 8.
Grease and dust a baking sheet with flour.

Sift the flour, pepper and salt into a large mixing
bowl, add the butter and rub in using your fingertips
until the mixture resembles coarse breadcrumbs.
Add the onion, cheese, egg and parsley and stir
well. Make a well in the centre and add the milk all
at once, stirring quickly and lightly to a soft dough.

Turn onto a lightly floured surface and knead just
enough to make a smooth surface and roll out to
¾ in (2 cm) thick. Stamp out rounds using a 2 in
(5 cm) cookie cutter.

Arrange on the baking sheet. Brush the tops with
the combined beaten egg and milk and then bake
for about 10 minutes, or until golden.

Honey scones

1 lb (450 g/4 cups)
self-raising (self-rising)
flour, plus extra for
dusting
1 teaspoon salt
2 oz (55 g) butter, plus extra
for greasing
1 egg
2 tablespoons honey
grated zest of 1 orange
12 fl oz (350 ml/1½ cups)
milk
1 egg beaten with 2 fl oz
(50 ml/¼ cup) milk,
to glaze
butter, to serve

makes 12–16

Preheat oven to 450°F/230°C/Gas mark 8. Grease
and dust a baking sheet with flour.

Sift flours and salt then, using fingertips, rub butter
into the flour mixture. Add egg, honey and zest.
Make a well in the centre and add the milk all at
once, stirring quickly and lightly to a soft dough.

Turn onto a lightly floured surface and knead just
enough to make a smooth surface and roll out to
¾ in (2 cm) thick. Stamp out rounds using a 2 in
(5 cm) cookie cutter.

Arrange on the baking sheet. Brush the tops with
the combined beaten egg and milk and then bake
for 10 minutes, or until golden.

Currant scones

8 oz (225 g/2 cups) plain
   (all-purpose) flour, plus
   extra for dusting
1¾ oz (45 g/¼ cup)
   granulated (white) sugar,
   plus extra for glazing
4 teaspoons baking powder
½ teaspoon salt
1½ oz (45 g) butter, chilled,
   plus extra for greasing
4 oz (115 g/½ cup) currants
1 egg
4 fl oz (120 ml/½ cup) milk,
   plus extra for glazing
butter, to serve

makes 12

Preheat the oven to 425°F/220°C/Gas mark 7.
Grease and dust a baking sheet with flour.

In a large bowl, combine the flour, sugar, baking
powder and salt. Rub in the butter using your
fingertips until the mixture resembles coarse
breadcrumbs. Stir in the currants. Make a well in
the centre.

In a small bowl, beat the egg. Stir in the milk. Pour
into the well. Stir with a fork to form a soft dough.

Turn onto a lightly floured surface and knead just
enough to make a smooth surface and roll out to
¾ in (2 cm) thick. Stamp out rounds using a 2 in
(5 cm) cookie cutter. Arrange on the prepared
baking sheet.

Brush the tops with milk and scatter with sugar. Bake
for 15 minutes until risen and browned slightly.

Ginger scones

8 oz (225 g/2 cups) plain
(all-purpose) flour, plus
extra for dusting
1 tablespoon sugar, plus
extra for dusting
2 teaspoons baking powder
½ teaspoon bicarbonate of
soda (baking soda)
¾ teaspoon salt
½ teaspoon groung cinnamon
(powder)
½ teaspoon ground ginger
1½ oz (40 g) butter, chilled,
plus extra for greasing
1 egg
4¼ oz (125 g/¼ cup)
molasses
2 fl oz (50 ml/¼ cup)
buttermilk or sour milk,
plus extra for glazing
butter, to serve

makes 12

Preheat the oven to 425°F/220°C/Gas mark 7.
Grease and dust a baking sheet with flour.

Put the flour, sugar, baking powder, bicarbonate of
soda, salt, cinnamon and ginger into a large bowl
and stir to combine. Rub in the butter until the
mixture resembles coarse breadcrumbs. Make a well
in the centre.

In a small bowl, beat the egg until frothy. Mix in the
molasses and buttermilk. Pour into the well. Stir with
a fork to make a soft dough.

Turn out onto a lightly floured surface. Knead
lightly until smooth. Roll out to a thickness of ¾ in
(2 cm) and stamp out rounds using a large cookie
cutter.

Brush the tops with milk. Dust with sugar. Score
each with a cross. Bake for 30 minutes, or until risen
and browned. Serve hot with butter.

Pecan meringues

3 egg whites
pinch of salt
1 teaspoon vanilla extract
5¼ oz (130 g/¾ cup) caster
   (superfine) sugar
8 oz (225 g/2 cups) pecans,
   chopped

makes 72

Preheat the oven to 350°F/180°C/Gas mark 4. Line several baking sheets with baking paper.

Beat the egg whites in a large glass grease-free bowl with an electric mixer until soft peaks form.

Add the salt, vanilla and sugar, beat for another 1 minute, then fold in the nuts.

Drop teaspoonfuls of mixture onto the prepared baking sheets, spacing them apart.

Bake for 2–3 minutes, turn off the oven and leave the meringues in the oven for 60 minutes. Use a spatula to ease the cookies off the paper.

Hazelnut macaroons

2 egg whites
2 oz (55 g/½ cup) icing
(confectioners') sugar,
sifted
4 oz (115 g/1 cup) ground
hazelnuts
1 teaspoon finely grated
orange zest
1 oz (30 g/¼ cup) flaked
almonds

makes 20

Preheat the oven to 400°F/200°C/Gas mark 6. Line
two baking sheets with baking paper.

Beat the egg whites in a grease-free bowl until soft
peaks form. Combine the remaining ingredients and
fold into egg whites.

Place spoonfuls of mixture on the prepared baking
sheets. Bake for 10–12 minutes or until golden.
Leave to set for a few minutes then transfer to wire
racks to go cold.

Coconut macaroons

oil, for greasing
5½ oz (160 g/1⅓ cups)
 desiccated dry
 unsweetened shredded)
 coconut
2½ oz (65 g/⅓ cup) sugar
2 tablespoons plain
 (all-purpose) flour
pinch of salt
2 egg whites, whisked
½ teaspoon almond extract

makes 20

Preheat the oven to 325°F/160°C/Gas mark 3.
Grease and line two baking sheets.

Combine the coconut, sugar, flour and salt in a
bowl.

In a clean, grease-free glass bowl, whisk the egg
whites until soft peaks form. Gently fold in the
coconut mixture with the almond extract.

Drop teaspoonfuls onto the baking sheet spaced
well apart. Bake for 15 minutes, or until the edges
turn brown. Remove from the sheets at once and
leave to cool on a wire rack.

muffins

Cheese & bacon muffins

8 oz (225 g/2 cups)
  self-raising (self-rising)
  flour
¼ teaspoon salt
1½ oz (40 g) mature
  Cheddar cheese, grated
  (shredded)
4–5 bacon rashers (slices),
  fried and crumbled
1 egg
8 fl oz (250 ml/1 cup) milk
2 fl oz (50 ml/¼ cup) olive oil

makes 12

Preheat the oven to 400°F/200°C/Gas mark 6. Line a muffin tray with paper cases.

Put the flour, baking powder, salt, cheese and bacon into a large bowl. Stir thoroughly. Make a well in the centre.

In another bowl, beat the milk and oil. Pour into the well. Stir only to moisten – the batter should be lumpy. Three-quarters fill the paper cases. Bake for 20–25 minutes until golden and cooked through. Serve warm.

Oat bran muffins

4 oz (115 g/1¼ cups) oat
   bran
4 oz (115 g/1 cup)
   self-raising (self-rising)
   flour
4 fl oz (120 ml/½ cup) milk
2 eggs
2 fl oz (50 ml/¼ cup) honey
3 tablespoons safflower oil

makes 10

Preheat the oven to 350°F/180°C/Gas mark 4. Line a muffin tray with paper cases.

Mix the oat bran and the flour in large bowl. Make a well in the centre

In another bowl, whisk the milk, eggs, honey and oil until smooth, pour into the well in the flour mixture. Stir until just mixed.

Bake for 15 minutes, or until a skewer inserted in centre comes out clean.

Raisin muffins

6 oz (150 g/1½ cups) plain
    (all-purpose) flour, sifted
2 teaspoons baking powder
½ teaspoon salt
2 oz (55 g/¼ cup) demerara
    (raw) sugar
5 oz (150 g/1 cup) raisins
6 fl oz (175 ml/¾ cup) milk
1 egg
1¼ oz (45 g) butter, melted

makes 12

Preheat the oven to 350°F/180°C/Gas mark 4. Line a muffin tray with paper cases.

In a medium bowl, sift together the flour, baking powder, salt and sugar. Stir in the raisins.

Whisk the egg, milk and melted butter together in a small bowl and whisk to combine. Pour the milk mixture into the dry ingredients and mix with a fork until just combined; do not over-mix.

Three-quarters fill the paper cases with batter. Bake for 20–25 minutes, or until muffins are cooked and golden. Turn onto a wire rack to cool.

Date muffins

9 oz (275 g/1½ cups)
 chopped dates
1 teaspoon bicarbonate of
 soda (baking soda)
7 oz (200 g/1¾ cups) plain
 (all-purpose) flour
1 teaspoon baking powder
½ teaspoon salt
2 oz (55 g/½ cup) chopped
 walnuts
2 eggs
6 oz (150 g/¾ cup) brown
 sugar, packed
2 fl oz (50 ml/¼ cup) oil
1 teaspoon vanilla extract

makes 16

Preheat the oven to 400°F/200°C/Gas mark 6. Line two muffin trays with paper cases.

Put the dates in a large bowl with 6 fl oz (175 ml/ ¾ cup) boiling water and the bicarbonate of soda. Mix once and set aside.

Combine the flour, baking powder, salt and walnuts in another bowl. Stir well. Set aside.

In a mixing bowl, beat the eggs until frothy. Slowly blend in the sugar, oil and vanilla. Stir in the date mixture. Pour in the dry ingredients and stir just to combine. The batter may be lumpy.

Three-quarters fill the paper cases, then bake for 20–25 minutes, or until cooked through.

Carrot & yogurt muffins

13 oz (375 g/3¼ cups)
    self-raising (self-rising)
    flour
½ teaspoon bicarbonate of
    soda (baking soda)
1 teaspoon mixed (apple pie)
    spice
3 oz (85 g) brown sugar
1 large carrot, grated
6 oz (175 g) sultanas (golden
    raisins)
7 oz (200 g) natural (plain)
    yogurt
8 fl oz (250 ml/1 cup) milk
1½ oz (40 g) butter, melted
2 eggs, lightly beaten

makes 24

Preheat the oven to 400°F/200°C/Gas mark 6. Line two muffin trays with paper cases.

Sift the flour, bicarbonate of soda and mixed spice into a large bowl. Add the sugar, carrot and sultanas and mix to combine.

In another bowl whisk together the yogurt, milk, melted butter and eggs. Stir yogurt mixture into flour mixture and mix until just combined.

Spoon batter into the paper cases and bake for 20 minutes, or until golden and cooked.

Carrot & cinnamon muffins

6 oz (150 g/1½ cups) plain
   (all-purpose) flour, sifted
2 teaspoons baking powder
½ teaspoon salt
1½ oz (40 g) sugar
1 teaspoon ground cinnamon
   (powder)
1 teaspoon ground nutmeg
5 oz (150 g/1 cup) grated
   (shredded) carrot
1¼ oz (35g/¼ cup) currants
1 egg
4 fl oz (120 ml/½ cup) milk
2½ oz (75 g) butter, melted

makes 12

Preheat the oven to 350°F/180°C/Gas mark 4. Line a muffin tray with paper cases.

In a medium bowl, sift together the flour, baking powder, salt, sugar and spices. Mix in the grated carrot and currants.

Whisk the egg, milk and melted butter together in a small bowl. Pour into dry ingredients and mix with a fork until just combined; do not over-mix.

Three-quarters fill the paper cases with batter. Bake for 20–25 minutes, or until muffins are golden. Turn out onto a wire rack to cool.

Carrot & sesame muffins

12 oz (350 g/3 cups)
  self-raising (self-rising)
  flour
½ teaspoon baking soda
1 teaspoon mixed (apple pie)
  spice
4 oz (115 g/½ cup) brown
  sugar
1 large carrot, grated
  (shredded)
4 tablespoons toasted sesame
  seeds
6 oz (175 g) sultanas (golden
  raisins)
8 fl oz (250 ml/1 cup)
  natural (plain) yogurt
8 fl oz (250 ml/1 cup) milk
1½ oz (40 g) butter, melted
3 egg whites, lightly beaten

makes 24

Preheat oven to 400°F/200°C/Gas mark 6. Line a
muffin tray with paper cases.

Sift the flour, baking soda and mixed spice into a
large bowl. Add the sugar, carrot, sesame seeds and
sultanas and mix to combine.

Whisk the yogurt, milk, butter and egg whites in a
bowl to combine. Stir the yogurt mixture into the
flour mixture and mix until just combined. Three-
quarters fill the paper cases with batter and bake for
20 minutes, or until golden and cooked.

Pumpkin muffins

6 oz (150 g/1½ cups) plain
    (all-purpose) flour
1 teaspoon baking powder
1 teaspoon bicarbonate of
    soda (baking soda)
½ teaspoon salt
½ teaspoon ground cinnamon
    (powder)
½ teaspoon freshly ground
    nutmeg
½ teaspoon ground ginger
4 oz (115 g/½ cup) raisins
1 egg
1¾ oz (45 g/¼ cup) sugar
2½ fl oz (75 ml/⅓ cup) olive
    oil
4½ oz (125 g/1 cup) cooked
    pumpkin
4 fl oz (120 ml/½ cup) milk
icing (confectioners') sugar,
    to dust

makes 12

Preheat the oven to 400°F/200°C/Gas mark 6. Line a muffin tray with paper cases.

Combine the flour, baking powder, bicarbonate of soda, salt, cinnamon, nutmeg, ginger and raisins in a large bowl. Stir thoroughly. Make a well in the centre.

In another bowl, beat the egg until frothy. Mix in the sugar, oil, pumpkin and milk. Pour into the well.

Stir to moisten. The batter will be lumpy. Three-quarters fill the paper cases, then bake for 15–20 minutes, or until golden and cooked through. Serve warm. Dust with icing sugar.

Raspberry muffins

4 oz (115 g/1 cup)
 wholemeal (whole-wheat)
 self-raising (self-rising)
 flour
4 oz (115 g/1 cup) white
 self-raising (self-rising)
 flour
1 oz (30 g/½ cup) wheat
 bran
½ teaspoon (bicarbonate of
 soda) baking soda
1 teaspoon ground ginger
6 fl oz (175 ml/¾ cup)
 buttermilk
2½ fl oz (75 ml/¹/₃ cup)
 orange juice concentrate
2 eggs
4 oz (115 g/²/₃ cup) fresh, or
 partly thawed, raspberries

makes 10

Preheat the oven to 350°F/180°C/Gas mark 4. Line a muffin tray with paper cases.

Sift the dry ingredients into a bowl. Return any bran to the bowl. Make a well in the centre.

In another bowl, beat together the buttermilk, orange juice and eggs. Pour into the well in the dry ingredients. Add the raspberries and mix until just combined – take care not to overmix. Divide between the paper cases.

Bake for 20–25 minutes, or until cooked when tested with a skewer.

Berry crumble muffins

4 oz (115 g/1 cup)
   self-raising (self-rising)
   flour, sifted
4 oz (115 g/1 cup) plain
   (all-purpose) flour, sifted
1 teaspoon baking powder
4 oz (115 g/½ cup) brown
   sugar
6 fl oz (175 ml/¾ cup) milk
2 fl oz (50 ml/¼ cup) canola
   oil
2 eggs, lightly beaten
4 oz (115 g/1 cup) frozen
   mixed berries

TOPPING
2 tablespoons plain
   (all-purpose) flour
1 oz (30 g) brown sugar
1 oz (30 g) butter, cubed

makes 12

Preheat oven to 350°F/180°C/Gas mark 4. Line a muffin tray with paper cases.

In a medium bowl sift together the flours and baking powder and stir in the sugar.

In a separate bowl, whisk the milk, oil and eggs together. Make a well in the centre of the dry ingredients and pour in the milk mixture.

Add the berries and mix until just combined.

To make the crumble topping, rub the butter into the flour with your fingertips until the mixture resembles breadcrumbs. Stir in the sugar and set aside.

Three-quarters fill the paper cases with batter then top with the crumble mixture.

Bake for 20–25 minutes or until a skewer, when inserted into the centre, comes out clean. Turn onto wire racks to cool.

Peanut butter muffins

6 oz (150 g/1½ cups) plain
    (all-purpose) flour
1¾ oz (45 g/¼ cup) sugar
1 tablespoon baking powder
½ teaspoon salt
3½ oz (90 g/1 cup) rolled
    oats
8 fl oz (250 ml/1 cup) milk
1 egg
4 oz (115 g/½ cup) smooth
    peanut butter
2 fl oz (50 ml/¼ cup) oil

makes 12

Preheat the oven to 400°F/200°C/Gas mark 6. Line a muffin tray with paper cases.

Combine the flour, sugar, baking powder and salt in a large bowl. Stir to mix. Make a well in the centre.

Combine the oats with the milk in a medium bowl.

Add the egg and peanut butter to the oats mixture and beat well. Add the oil and stir through. Pour into the well, then stir just enough to moisten. Three-quarters fill the paper cases, then bake for 15–20 minutes, or until golden and cooked through. Serve warm.

Pecan & almond cakes

2 eggs, separated
3½ oz (100 g/½ cup) caster
  (superfine) sugar
few drops vanilla extract
2 oz (55 g/½ cup plain)
  (all-purpose) flour
1 teaspoon baking powder
1 oz (30 g/¼ cup) mixed
  pecans and almonds,
  chopped
2 tablespoons icing
  (confectioners') sugar

makes 12

Preheat the oven to 300°F/150°C/Gas mark 2. Line a muffin tray with paper cases.

Whisk the egg yolks with the sugar in a large bowl until thick and pale. Gently stir in the vanilla. Sift the flour and baking powder over the egg and sugar mixture, then fold in.

In a clean grease-free bowl, whisk the egg whites until stiff then fold gently into the egg mixture. Carefully fold the nuts into the mixture.

Divide among the paper cases and bake for 15 minutes, or until golden. Dust with icing sugar and serve warm.

Jaffa pecan cakes

3½ oz (100 g) dark
    (bittersweet) chocolate,
    chopped
4 oz (115 g) butter
2 eggs
2 tablespoons orange liqueur
finely grated (shredded) zest
    of ½ orange
1¾ oz (45 g/¼ cup) caster
    (superfine) sugar
2 oz (60 g) pecans, chopped
2 oz (55 g/½ cup) plain
    (all-purpose) flour, sifted
18 pecan halves

makes 18

Preheat the oven to 350°F/180°C/Gas mark 4. Line two muffin trays with paper cases.

Put the chopped chocolate and butter in a heatproof bowl set over a saucepan of simmering water and leave until the chocolate and butter melt, stirring occasionally. Remove the bowl from the heat and set aside to cool slightly.

In a bowl, beat the eggs, then stir in the liqueur, orange zest, sugar and pecans. Fold in the chocolate mixture and mix to combine. Fold in the flour.

Three-quarters fill the paper cases with batter, top with a pecan half and bake for 20 minutes, or until the cakes are cooked through. Leave to cool on a wire rack.

cookies

Butter cookies

4 oz (115 g) butter, plus
  extra for greasing
4 oz (115 g) ghee
8¾ oz (245 g/1¼ cups)
  caster (superfine) sugar
½ teaspoon ground cinnamon
  (powder)
3 eggs
2½ fl oz (75 ml/¹/₃ cup)
  brandy
1½ teaspoons baking powder
1 lb–1 lb 4 oz (4–5 cups)
  plain (all-purpose) flour
sesame seeds
egg glaze made by whisking
  1 egg with 2 tablespoons
  of milk

makes about 48

Preheat the oven to 375°F/190°C/Gas mark 5.
Grease several baking sheets.

In a large bowl, cream the butter, ghee and sugar
until light and fluffy. Add the cinnamon and eggs,
beating the mixture well.

Add the brandy and baking powder, then add the
flour in batches. Add as much as is needed to make
a stiff (not dry) dough. Test to see if the dough is the
correct consistency by rolling a little in your hands
– if it is not sticky, and rolls well, enough flour has
been added.

Shape pieces of dough into slim pencil-shapes, roll
in sesame seeds, then form into scrolls. Place on
the prepared baking sheets. Brush with egg glaze
and bake for 15–20 minutes. Leave to set for a few
minutes then turn out onto a wire rack to go cold.

Sweet cinnamon bows

6 oz (150 g/1½ cups) plain
(all-purpose) flour, plus
extra for dusting
1¾ oz (45 g/¼ cup) caster
(superfine) sugar
2 teaspoons ground
cinnamon (powder)
4 oz (115 g/½ cup) cream
cheese, at room
temperature
4 oz (115 g/½ cup) unsalted
butter, at room
temperature
icing (confectioners') sugar,
sifted, to dust

makes 50

Sift the flour, sugar and cinnamon into a large mixing bowl. Add the cream cheese and butter and beat until just combined – take care not to overmix the dough.

Turn the dough out onto a lightly floured surface, gather into a ball and knead briefly. Wrap in cling wrap (cling film) and refrigerate for at least 1 hour.

Line several baking sheets with baking paper.

Roll out the dough on a lightly floured surface to ⅛ in (3 mm) thick. Cut into strips ½ in (12 mm) wide and 8 in (20 cm) long. Shape each strip into a bow and place on the prepared baking sheets. Cover and refrigerate for 15 minutes.

Preheat oven to 375°F/190°C/Gas mark 5.

Bake for 5 minutes, then reduce the oven temperature to 300°F/150°C/Gas mark 2 and bake for 10–15 minutes or until puffed and golden brown. Transfer to wire racks to cool. Dust with icing sugar.

Cinnamon cookies

8 oz (225 g) butter, softened,
   plus extra for greasing
4 oz (115 g) caster
   (superfine) sugar
1 teaspoon vanilla extract
12 oz (350 g/3 cups) plain
   (all-purpose) flour
2 teaspoons ground
   cinnamon (powder)
salt
6 oz (150 g/1½ cups) icing
   (confectioners') sugar

makes 24

In a bowl, beat together the butter, sugar and vanilla extract. Stir in the flour, 1 teaspoon of cinnamon and a pinch of salt to make a soft dough. Cover and refrigerate for 1 hour.

Preheat oven to 350°F/180°C/Gas mark 4. Grease two baking sheets.

Form mixture into 1 in (2.5 cm) balls and place on a prepared baking sheet, leaving space between each one. Bake for 15 minutes. Leave to set on the baking sheets for a few minutes, then transfer to a wire rack to cool.

Mix together the icing sugar and remaining cinnamon and dust over the cookies before serving.

Ginger bites

1 oz (30 g) butter, plus extra
   for greasing
1¾ oz (45 g/¼ cup) sugar
1 egg
2 oz (55 g/½ cup) plain
   (all-purpose) wholemeal
   (whole-wheat) flour, sifted
2 oz (55 g/½ cup) plain
   (all-purpose) flour, sifted
2 teaspoons ground ginger
1 tablespoon glacé
   (crystallized) ginger
½ teaspoon ground nutmeg
¼ teaspoon ground cloves
2 tablespoons molasses or
   golden (light corn) syrup,
   warmed

makes 28

Beat the butter and sugar in a mixing bowl until
light and fluffy. Beat in the egg, then stir in the
remaining ingredients. Cover and refrigerate for
1 hour.

Preheat the oven to 325°F/160°C/Gas mark 3.
Grease two or three baking sheets.

Roll teaspoons of mixture into balls. Place on the
prepared baking sheets and flatten slightly. Bake for
10–12 minutes, or until golden.

Chewy coffee cookies

4 oz (115 g/½ cup) butter, at
   room temperature
4 oz (115 g/½ cup) brown
   sugar
1 large egg, plus 1 yolk
2 tablespoons coffee liqueur
4½ oz (125 g/⅓ cup)
   molasses
3 tablespoons instant coffee
   powder or granules
10 oz (275 g/2½ cups) plain
   (all-purpose) flour
1 teaspoon ground cinnamon
   (powder)
½ teaspoon ground
   cardamom
2 teaspoons bicarbonate soda
   (baking soda)
2 oz (55 g/½ cup) icing
   (confectioners') sugar

makes 25

Preheat the oven to 350°F/180°C/Gas mark 4.
Lightly grease two or three baking sheets.

Cream the butter and brown sugar until light and
fluffy in a mixing bowl. Add the egg, egg yolk,
liqueur and molasses, and beat together.

Sift the coffee, flour, spices and baking soda into the
egg mixture and fold in gently.

Roll tablespoons of the mixture into ballsthen roll
each in the icing sugar. Arrange on the prepared
baking sheets and bake for 12–14 minutes.

Coffee kisses

9 oz (250 g) butter, at room
  temperature, plus extra for
  greasing
2 oz (55 g/½ cup) icing
  (confectioners') sugar,
  sifted, plus extra for
  dusting
2 teaspoons instant coffee
  powder or granules
  dissolved in 1 tablespoon
  hot water, then cooled
8 oz (225 g/2 cups) plain
  (all-purpose) flour, sifted
2 oz (55 g) dark (bittersweet)
  chocolate, melted

makes 25

Preheat the oven to 350°F/180°C/Gas mark 4.
Grease two baking sheets.

Beat the butter and icing sugar together in a mixing
bowl until light and fluffy. Stir in the coffee and then
the flour.

Spoon the mixture into a piping bag fitted with a
medium star nozzle and pipe 2 cm (¾ in) rounds of
mixture 2 cm (¾ in) apart on the prepared baking
sheets.

Bake for 10–12 minutes, or until lightly browned.
Leave to set for 5 minutes before turning out onto a
wire rack to cool completely.

Join the cookies with a little melted chocolate, then
dust with icing sugar.

Pecan coffee drizzles

5 teaspoons instant coffee
    powder or granules
3½ oz (100 g) unsalted
    butter, at room
    temperature, plus extra for
    greasing
3½ oz (100 g) brown sugar
1 egg, lightly beaten
11 oz (300 g) plain
    (all-purpose flour
1 teaspoon baking powder
2½ oz (75 g) pecans, roughly
    chopped
2½ oz (65 g) milk chocolate
2 tablespoons confectioners'
    (icing) sugar

makes 20

Dissolve 4 teaspoons of the coffee in 1 tablespoon boiling water. Set aside to cool slightly.

Beat together the butter and sugar in a bowl until light and creamy, add the egg and beat well. Add the flour, baking powder and coffee mixture, then work together with your hands until the dough is smooth. Refrigerate for 10 minutes.

Preheat the oven to 350°F/180°C/Gas mark 4. Lightly grease two baking sheets.

Roll out half of the mixture between two sheets of baking paper to ¼ in (6 mm) thick. Stamp out rounds using a 2½ in (6 cm) cookie cutter. Repeat with the remaining dough.

Place the cookies on the prepared baking trays and bake for 10 minutes. Turn out on to a wire rack and scatter with nuts.

Melt the chocolate. Stir in the remaining coffee and the icing sugar and stir to combine. Drizzle over the cooled cookies. Leave to set.

Butterscotch rolls

2 oz (55 g) butter, softened,
plus 1½ oz (40 g) chilled
6 oz (175 g/¾ cup) brown
sugar, packed
8 oz (225 g/2 cups) plain
(all-purpose) flour, plus
extra for dusting
2 tablespoons sugar
4 teaspoons baking powder
1 teaspoon salt
6 fl oz (175 ml/¾ cup) milk
1½ oz (40 g/⅓ cup) chopped
nuts

makes 12

Preheat the oven to 425°F/220°C/Gas mark 7.
Grease an 8 in (20 cm) square cake tin (pan).

In a mixing bowl, beat the softened butter and
brown sugar together until light and fluffy. Set aside.

In a large bowl, combine the flour, sugar, baking
powder and salt. Rub in the chilled butter until
crumbly using your fingertips. Make a well in
the centre.

Pour the milk into the well. Stir to make a soft
dough. Knead 8–10 times. Roll out on a lightly
floured surface to a 9–10 in (23–25 cm) square.
Spread with the brown sugar mixture. Scatter with
chopped nuts.

Roll up the dough as a Swiss roll (jelly roll). Pinch
the edge to seal. Cut into 12 slices. Arrange in the
prepared tin. Bake for 15–20 minutes. Leave to
stand for a few minutes then turn out on to a wire
rack to go cold.

Hazelnut shortbreads

9 oz (250 g) butter, diced,
    plus extra for greasing
6 oz (150 g/1½ cups) plain
    (all-purpose) flour, sifted,
    plus extra for dusting
1½ oz (40 g) ground
    hazelnuts (meal)
1½ oz (40 g) ground rice
1¾ oz (45 g/¼ cup) caster
    (superfine) sugar
3½ oz (100 g) chocolate,
    melted

makes 40

Preheat the oven to 325°F/160°C/Gas mark 3.
Grease two or three baking sheets.

Put the butter, flour, ground hazelnuts and ground
rice in a food processor and process until the
mixture resembles coarse breadcrumbs. Add the
sugar and process again to combine.

Turn the mixture out onto a floured surface and
knead lightly to make a pliable dough. Flatten
between sheets of baking paper and roll out to
¼ in (6 mm) thick. Using a 2 in (5 cm) fluted cookie
cutter, stamp out rounds of dough.

Arrange the cookies 1 in (2.5 cm) apart on the
prepared baking sheets. Bake for 10–15 minutes, or
until lightly browned. Leave to set for 2–3 minutes
before transferring to wire racks to cool.

Tip the melted chocolate in a plastic food bag,
snip off one corner and pipe lines across each
shortbread before serving.

Almond biscotti

oil, for greasing
2 large eggs
3½ oz (100 g/½ cup) caster
    (superfine) sugar
1 teaspoon vanilla extract
1 teaspoon grated orange
    zest
6½ oz (180 g/1⅔ cups) plain
    (all-purpose) flour, plus
    extra for dusting
½ teaspoon baking powder
¾ cup blanched almonds,
    lightly toasted
egg white, for glazing

makes 30

Preheat the oven to 350°F/180°C/Gas mark 4. Grease two baking sheets and dust with flour.

In a mixing bowl, beat the eggs, sugar, vanilla extract and orange zest until thick and creamy.

Sift the flour and baking powder into the egg mixture and fold in with the almonds.

Knead on a floured surface until smooth. Divide dough in half. Shape each piece into a log about 2 in (5 cm) wide and 1 in (2. 5cm) thick. Place on a baking sheet. Brush with egg white.

Bake for 30 minutes, or until firm. Cool for 10 minutes. Cut each log diagonally into 1 cm (³/₈ in) thick slices. Place on the baking trays. Bake for 20–30 minutes, or until dry and crisp. Cool on wire racks.

Peanut butter
& honey cookies

6 oz (150 g/¾ cup) crunchy
    peanut butter
5½ oz (160 g/²/₃ cup honey
1 egg, lightly beaten
4 oz (115 g/1 cup) plain
    (all-purpose) flour, sifted
1¾ oz (50 g/½ cup) rolled
    oats
2 oz (55 g/¹/₃ cup) sultanas
    (golden raisins)

makes 30

Preheat the oven to 325°F/160°C/Gas mark 3. Line two or three baking sheets with baking paper.

Put the peanut butter and honey in a saucepan and place over gentle heat. Stir until soft and combined. Leave to coool slightly then stir in the beaten egg. Fold in the remaining ingredients.

Shape teaspoons of mixture into balls. Arrange on the prepared trays leaving space between each. Press lightly with a fork. Bake for 12 minutes, or until golden. Leave to set for a few minutes before turning out onto a wire rack to go cold.

Pistachio oat bran bakes

2 oz (55 g) butter, plus extra
    for greasing
4½ oz (125 g/²/₃ cup) sugar
1 teaspoon vanilla extract
½ teaspoon bicarbonate of
    soda (baking soda)
½ teaspoon cream of tartar
4 oz (115 g/1 cup) plain
    (all-purpose) flour
1¾ oz (50 g/½ cup) oat bran
2½ fl oz (75 ml/¹/₃ cup)
    buttermilk
2 oz (55 g/½ cup) chopped
    pistachios

makes about 30

Preheat the oven to 400°F/200°C/Gas mark 6.
Grease two baking sheets.

Combine the butter and sugar in a mixing bowl,
beat until creamy. Add the vanilla, bicarbonate of
soda and cream of tartar. Mix in well.

Sift over the flour and oat bran in batches,
alternating withthe buttermilk, and mixing well after
each addition. Fold in half the pistachios.

Roll teaspoons of the mixture, flatten slightly then
press one side into the remaining pistachios. Place
pistachio-side up on the prepared baking sheets.
Bake until golden, about 10 minutes.

Leave to set for 2 minutes, then turn out on to a wire
rack to cool completely.

Oatmeal cookies

4 oz (115 g/½ cup) butter
8 oz (200 g/1 cup) brown
  sugar
2 eggs
2 ripe bananas, mashed
3 teaspoons vanilla extract
10 oz (275 g/2½ cups) plain
  (all-purpose) flour
5¼ oz (150 g/1½ cups)
  rolled oats
½ teaspoon baking powder
2 oz (55 g/½ cup) chopped
  hazelnuts

makes about 40

Preheat the oven to 350°F/180°C/Gas mark 4.
Grease two baking sheets.

Cream the butter and sugar in a large mixing bowl
until soft and fluffy. Add the eggs and beat well.
Add the banana and vanilla.

Sift the flour into another bowl, add the oats and
baking powder, then gradually, add the flour
mixture and the milk to the banana mixture. Stir in
the hazelnuts.

Place tablespoons of mixture onto the prepared
baking sheets. Bake for 10 minutes, or until slightly
browned around the edges. Leave to set for a few
minutes before turning out to cool on a wire rack.

Florentines

4 oz (115 g/½ cup) butter, at
room temperature
3½ oz (100 g/½ cup) sugar
5 tablespoons golden (light
corn) syrup
1 oz (30 g/¼ cup) plain
(all-purpose) flour
4 oz (115 g/1 cup) sliced
(flaked) almonds
4 oz (115 g/½ cup) glacé
cherries, chopped
2 oz (55 g/½ cup) walnuts,
chopped
1½ oz (40 g/¼ cup) mixed
peel, chopped
5 oz (150 g) milk chocolate

makes 20

Preheat the oven to 350°F/180°C/Gas mark 4. Line four baking sheets with baking paper.

Cream the butter and sugar in a large bowl until soft and fluffy. Beat in the golden syrup. Sift in the flour an stir to combine. Add the almonds, cherries, walnuts and mixed peel and mix well.

Place tablespoonfuls of the mixture onto the prepared baking sheets, leaving plenty of room for the cookies to spread. Using a knife, press each one out as flat and round as possible. Cook no more than 4 or 5 to a tray.

Bake for 10 minutes, or until golden brown. Leave to set for 5 minutes before transferring to a wire rack to go cold.

Meanwhile, melt the chocolate in a bowl set over a pan (pot) of simmering water. When the florentines are cold, coat with melted chocolate on their flat sides.

cakes & tea breads

Victoria sandwich cake

4 eggs
5¼ oz (150 g/¾ cup) caster
    (superfine) sugar
4 oz (115 g/1 cup)
    self-raising (self-rising)
    flour
1 tablespoon cornflour
    (cornstarch)
½ oz (15 g) butter, melted
1 tablespoon icing
    (confectioners') sugar,
    sifted, for dusting

FILLING

5 oz (150 g/½ cup)
    strawberry jam (jelly)
4 fl oz (120 ml/½ cup)
    double (heavy) cream,
    whipped

makes 1 cake

Preheat the oven to 350°F/180°C/Gas mark 4. Grease and line two 8 in (20 cm) round cake tins (pans).

Beat the eggs in a mixing bowl until thick and creamy. Gradually beat in the sugar and continue until thick and the sugar has dissolved. This will take about 10 minutes.

Sift the flour and cornflour together over the egg mixture, then fold in. Stir in 2½ fl oz (75 ml/⅓ cup warm water and the melted butter.

Divide the batter between the prepared cake tins.

Bake for 20–25 minutes, or until the cakes shrink slightly from the sides of tins and spring back when touched with the fingertips. Stand cakes in tins for 5 minutes before turning out onto wire racks to cool.

To assemble, spread one cake with jam, then top with whipped cream and the remaining sponge cake. Just prior to serving, dust cake with icing sugar.

Flourless poppy seed cake

4 large eggs, separated
4½ oz (125 g) butter,
  softened
grated zest of 1 lemon
3½ oz (100 g) icing
  (confectioners') sugar
2 tablespoons unsweetened
  cocoa powder
1¾ oz (55 g) caster
  (superfine) sugar
5½ oz (160 g) poppy seeds,
  ground
extra icing (confectioners')
  sugar, to serve

makes 1 cake

Preheat the oven to 350°F/180°C/Gas mark 4.
Grease and line a 24 cm (9½ in) round cake tin (pan).
Set aside.

In the bowl of an electric mixer, beat the egg yolks,
butter, lemon zest and icing sugar until thick and
smooth, about 5 minutes. Fold in the cocoa and
mix well.

Meanwhile, beat the egg whites in another clean
grease-free bowl until 'foamy'. Scatter over the
caster sugar and continue beating until thick and
glossy.

Mix the poppy seeds into the yolk mixture, then add
the egg whites and combine gently.

Spoon the batter into the prepared tin and smooth
the top. Bake for 1 hour 10 minutes, or until a
skewer inserted into the centre comes out clean.
Allow to cool in the tin, then turn out onto a serving
plate. Dust with icing sugar.

Orange poppy seed cake

4 tablespoons poppy seeds
2 fl oz (50 ml/¼ cup) orange
  juice
4 oz (115 g) natural (plain)
  yogurt
7 oz (200 g) butter, softened,
  plus extra for greasing
1 tablespoon finely grated
  orange zest
7 oz (200 g/1 cup) caster
  (superfine) sugar
3 eggs
8 oz (225 g/2 cups)
  self-raising (self-rising)
  flour, sifted, plus extra for
  dusting
2 tablespoons orange
  marmalade, warmed, to
  glaze

makes 1 cake

Preheat the oven to 350°F/180°C/Gas mark 4.
Grease an 8 in (20 cm) fluted ring tin and dust lightly
with flour.

Place the poppy seeds, orange juice and yogurt into
a bowl, mix to combine and set aside for 1 hour.

Put the butter and orange zest in a bowl and beat
until light and fluffy. Gradually add the sugar,
beating well until the mixture is creamy.

Add the eggs one at a time, beating well after each
addition. Fold the flour and poppy seed mixture,
alternately, into the butter mixture.

Pour the batter into the prepared tin. Bake for
35–40 minutes, or until cooked when tested with a
skewer. Leave to stand for 5 minutes before turning
out onto a wire rack to cool completely. Brush with
orange marmalade, before serving.

Cherry & almond cake

8 oz (225 g/1 cup) butter
7 oz (200 g/1 cup caster
   (superfine) sugar
2 eggs
8 oz (225 g/2 cups) plain
   (all-purpose) flour
½ teaspoon ground cinnamon
   (powder)
½ teaspoon ground cloves
8 oz (224 g/2 cups) ground
   almonds (almond meal)
1 tablespoon gin

FILLING & TOPPING

5 tablespoons cherry jam
   (jelly)
8 fl oz (250 ml/1 cup)
   whipped cream

makes 1 cake

Preheat the oven to 350°F/180°C/Gas mark 4. Grease and line an 8 in (20 cm) round deep cake tin (pan).

Beat the butter until soft, add the sugar and continue beating until light and fluffy. Add the eggs, one at a time, beating well after each addition.

Sift the flour, cinnamon, cloves and almonds together. Add to the creamed mixture with the gin, mixing until well combined.

Tip half the batter into the prepared tin. Spread evenly with 3 tablespoons of the jam, then spread pour the remaining cake batter on top.

Bake for 1 hour, or until pale golden. Leave to set in the tin for 5 minutes, then turn out onto a wire rack to cool.

Spread the top of the cake with cream and decorate with the remaining jam.

Strawberry shortbreads

8 oz (225 g/2 cups) butter
3½ oz (100 g/½ cup)
  superfine (caster) sugar
2 eggs, lightly beaten
1 teaspoon vanilla extract
6 oz (150 g/1½ cups) plain
  (all-purpose) flour
2 oz (55 g/½ cup) cornflour
  (cornstarch)
1 tablespoon baking powder

FILLING

8 fl oz (250 ml/1 cup) milk
½ teaspoon vanilla extract
2 oz (65 g/¹/₃ cup) superfine
  (caster) sugar
3 egg yolks
2 tablespoons cornstarch
  (cornflour)
8 fl oz (250 ml/1 cup)·
  whipped cream
5 oz (150 g/1 cup) sliced
  strawberries, plus a
  handful of whole
  strawberries, to decorate

makes 1 cake

Preheat the oven 350°F/180°C/Gas mark 4. Grease and line two 7 in (18 cm) sandwich tins (pans),

In a bowl, ceam the butter and sugar until light and fluffy. Add the eggs and vanilla and beat thoroughly.

Sift the flour, cornstarch and baking powder onto the egg mixture and beat well. Divide the batter between the prepared tins and bake for 20 minutes, or until cooked through. Leave to set for a few minutes, then turn out on to a wire rack to go cold.

To make the custard, slowly bring the milk and vanilla to the boil in a heavy pan.

Meanwhile, beat the sugar and eggs together in a bowl until the mixture is thick and creamy, and leaves a trail when the beaters are lifted. Fold in the cornstarch. Then pour the hot milk onto the egg mixture, beating well.

Return the mixture to the pan and reheat, stirring constantly. Boil for 1 minute, then pour into a bowl and cover with a sheet of baking paper until cold.

Spread the custard on one cake. Top with sliced strawberries and some of the cream. Add the other cake and decorate with strawberries and cream.

Coffee sandwich cake

9 oz (250 g) butter, at room
  temperature
7 oz (225 g/1 cup) caster
  (superfine) sugar
6 eggs, lightly beaten
8 oz (225 g/2 cups)
  self-raising (self-rising)
  flour, sifted

ICING
2¼ oz (60 g) butter, softened
3 oz (85 g/¾ cup) icing
  (confectioners') sugar,
  sifted
½ teaspoon ground cinnamon
  powder
2 teaspoons instant coffee
  dissolved in 2 teaspoons
  hot water, then cooled

FILLING
1 tablespoon coffee-flavoured
  liqueur
4 fl oz (120 ml/½ cup)
  double (heavy) cream,
  whipped

Makes 1 cake

Preheat the oven to 325°F/160°C/Gas mark 3.
Grease and line two 7 in (18 cm) sandwich tins
(pans).

Cream the butter and sugar in a large bowl until
light and fluffy. Add the eggs, one at a time and
beat well. Sift over the flour and mix to combine.

Divide the batter between the prepared tins and
bake for 30–35 minutes, or until golden. Leave to set
in the tin for a few minuts then turn out on to a wire
rack to go cold.

Meanwhile, to make the icing, beat the butter, icing
sugar, cinnamon and coffee in a large bowl until
light and fluffy.

To make the filling, fold the liqueur into the
whipped cream.

Spread the filling over one cake and top with the
remaining cake. Spread the icing over the top of
the cake.

Pear upside-down cake

¼ cup demerara (raw) sugar
2 x 15 oz (440 g) cans pear
  halves, drained but
  reserving 8 fl oz
  (250 ml/1 cup) syrup
8 oz (225 g/1 cup) butter,
  softened
8 oz (225 g/2 cups)
  self-raising (self-rising)
  flour
7 oz (200 g/1 cup) caster
  (superfine) sugar
4 eggs
4 oz (115 g/1 cup) chopped
  walnuts
2 fl oz (50 ml/¼ cup) maple
  syrup
Cream or ice cream, to serve

Makes 1 cake

Preheat the oven to 350°F/180°C/Gas mark 4.
Grease and line a deep round 9 in (23 cm) cake tin
(pan).

Scatter the base of the cake tin with the demerara
sugar. Cut each pear halves in half and arrange cut-
side up, on top.

Bea the butter, flour, sugar and eggs in a food
processor until smooth. Stir in the walnuts.

Carefully spoon the batter over the fruit in the tin.
Bake for 1–1¼ hours, or until cooked through.

Pour the maple syrup and the reserved pear juice
into a saucepan and place over a medium heat. Stir
well then cook until the syrup is reduced by half.

Turn the cake out onto a serving plate and pour
over the syrup. Serve hot or cold with cream or
ice cream.

Apple cake

5 oz (150 g) butter
7 oz (200 g) sugar
3 eggs, separated
7 oz (225 g/1¾ cups) plain
   (all-purpose) flour
2 teaspoons baking powder
2 tablespoons ground
   almonds (almond meal)
pinch of salt
¼ teaspoon nutmeg
¼ teaspoon ground cinnamon
   powder
6 cooking apples, peeled,
   cored and sliced and
   brushed with 2
   tablespoons lemon juice

Makes 1 cake

Preheat the oven to 350°F/180°C/Gas mark 4.
Grease and line a 9 in (23 cm) round cake tin (pan).

Beat the butter and 5 oz (150 g) of the sugar
together, in a mixing bowl, until thick and pale. Add
the egg yolks one at a time, beating well after each
addition.

In another clean, grease-free bowl, whisk the egg
whites until firm peaks form.

In another bowl, mix the flour, baking powder,
ground almonds, salt and spices.

Add half the egg whites and flour mixture to the
batter and whisk together carefully. Repeat with the
remaining ingredients and mix well.

Pour the batter into the prepared tin. Press the
apple slices into the batter in a circular pattern, dust
with the remaining sugar. Bake for 50 minutes, until
golden. Leave to set in the tin for 10 minutes, then
turn out on to a wire rack to go cold.

Spiced apple cake

2 cooking apples, cored,
    peeled and sliced
4 oz (115 g) butter
8 oz (225 g/1 cup) demerara
    (raw) sugar
2 eggs
4 oz (115 g/1 cup)
    self-raising (self-rising)
    flour
4 oz (115 g/1 cup)
    wholemeal (whole-wheat)
    flour
½ teaspoon bicarbonate of
    soda (baking soda)
1½ teaspoons mixed (apple
    pie) spice
1 oz (30 g) walnuts, chopped
2 oz (60 g) raisins, chopped
6 fl oz (175 ml/¾ cup)
    double (heavy) cream,
    whipped
icing (confectioners') sugar,
    sifted, for dusting

makes 1 cake

Preheat the oven to 350°F/180°C/Gas mark 4.
Grease and line a 9 in (23 cm) round cake tin (pan).

Put the apples and 6 fl oz (175 ml/¾ cup) water in
a saucepan and cook over a medium heat until
tender. Place in a food processor or blender and
process until smooth. Set aside to cool.

Put the butter and sugar in a mixing bowl and beat
until light and fluffy. Add the eggs, one at a time,
beating well after each addition.

Sift together the flours, bicarbonate of soda and
1 teaspoon of the mixed spice into a bowl. Return
the husks to the bowl. Mix the flour mixture and the
apple purée, alternately, into butter mixture, then
stir in the walnuts and raisins.

Tip the batter into the prepared tin. Bake for 40
minutes, or until cooked through. Allow to cool in
the tin for 5 minutes before turning onto a wire rack
to cool completely.

Split the cake in half horizontally, spread the base
with cream, then top with the other cake half and
dust with the remaining mixed spice and icing sugar.

Banana & date loaf

8 oz (225 g/2 cups)
   self-rising (self-raising)
   flour
1 teaspoon baking soda
salt
1 teaspoon ground cinnamon
   (powder)
3½ oz (100 g/½ cup) caster
   (superfine) sugar
4 oz (115 g/¾ cup) fresh
   dates, pitted and chopped
2 eggs, lightly beaten
8 fl oz (250 ml/1 cup) milk
2 ripe bananas, mashed

makes 1 loaf

Preheat the oven to 350°F/180°C/Gas mark 4.
Grease and line a 23 x 13 cm (9 x 5 in) loaf tin (pan).

Sift the flour, baking soda, pinch of salt and
cinnamon into a large bowl. Stir in the sugar and
dates.

In another bowl, combine the eggs, milk and
bananas in a bowl and whisk until well combined.
Stir the egg mixture into the dry ingredients until
well combined.

Pour the batter into the prepared tin. Bake for
40–45 minutes, then test with a skewer to make sure
the bread is baked.

Leave to set in the tin for 10 minutes, then turn out
onto a wire rack to cool.

Banana bread

4 oz (115 g) butter, at room
   temperature
7 oz (225 g/1 cup) superfine
   (caster) sugar
2 eggs, lightly beaten
3 ripe bananas, peeled
2 tablespoons honey
2 tablespoons lemon juice
1 teaspoon vanilla extract
6 oz (150 g/1½ cups)
   self-rising (self-raising)
   flour, sifted
½ teaspoon baking soda
1 teaspoon ground cinnamon
   (powder)
2 oz (55 g/½ cup) almond
   meal (ground almonds)

makes 1 loaf

Preheat the oven to 350°F/180°C/Gas mark 4.
Grease a 9 x 6 in (23 x 15 cm) loaf tin (pan).

Put the butter and sugar in a mixing bowl. Beat with
an electric beater until light and creamy. Add the
eggs and beat until combined.

In another bowl, combine the bananas, honey,
lemon juice and vanilla and blend until smooth.

Stir the banana mixture into the batter and mix until
well combined. Gently fold in in the flour, baking
soda, cinnamon and almonds.

Tip into the prepared tin and bake for 50–60
minutes or until cooked through. Leave to set for
5 minutes then turn out on a wire rack to go cold.
Serve sliced and buttered.

Holiday spice bread

4 oz (115 g/1 cup) almonds,
  coarsely chopped
4 oz (115 g/½ cup) sultanas
  (golden raisins)
¼ teaspoon salt
¼ teaspoon nutmeg
1 teaspoon ground ginger
1½ teaspoon ground
  cinnamon (powder)
1 teaspoon anise seed
¼ teaspoon ground cloves
1½ teaspoons dried orange
  zest, grated
3 teaspoons baking powder
2 oz (55 g/¼ cup) brown
  sugar
8 fl oz (250 ml/1 cup) honey
1 oz (30 g) butter, melted
1 large egg, lightly beaten
2½ fl oz (75 ml/¹/₃ cup) rum
4 oz (115 g/1 cup) strong
  white bread flour, plus
  extra for dusting
4 oz (115 g/1 cup) rye flour
4 oz (115 g/1 cup)
  wholemeal (whole-wheat)
  flour

makes 1 loaf

Preheat the oven to 400°F/200°C/Gas mark 6.
Grease a 6 x 10 in (15 x 25 cm) loaf tin (pan). Dust
the base and sides with flour, and shake out
the excess.

In a large mixing bowl, combine the almonds,
sultanas, salt, nutmeg, ginger, cinnamon, anise
seed, cloves, orange and baking powder.

Bring 8 fl oz (250 ml/1 cup) water to a boil in a pan
over moderate heat. Add the honey and stir to
dissolve. Add the brown sugar and stir to dissolve.
Remove from the heat, set aside for 5 minutes.

Add the egg and rum to the honey and sugar
mixture and whisk to blend. Add to the spice
mixture and stir to blend. Add the flours and stir
until just absorbed.

Transfer the dough to the prepared tin and bake
for 10 minutes. Reduce heat to 350°F/180°C/
Gas mark 4 and bake for 30 minute, or until a cake
tester inserted into the centre comes out clean.

Leave to set in the tin for 5 minutes, before turning out
onto a wire rack to go cold.

Blueberry pecan loaf

4 oz (115 g/1 cup)
  wholemeal (whole-wheat)
  flour
4 oz (115 g/1 cup) plain
  (all-purpose) flour
1½ teaspoons baking powder
1 teaspoon salt
½ teaspoon bicarbonate of
  soda (baking soda)
1½ oz (45 g) butter
6 fl oz (175 ml/¾ cup)
  natural (plain) yogurt
1 tablespoon grated lemon
  zest
2 eggs
4 oz (115 g/1 cup)
  blueberries
4 oz (115 g/1 cup) chopped
  pecans

makes 1 loaf

Preheat the oven to 350°F/180°C/Gas mark 4. Grease and line a 1 lb (450 g) loaf tin (pan).

Sift the flours, baking powder, salt and bicarbonate of soda into the bowl of a food processor. Add the butter, and process until the mixture resembles coarse breadcrumbs.

Combine the yogurt, lemon zest and eggs in a separate bowl, mix well. Add to the processor and blend just long enough to moisten. Add the blueberries and nuts and stir through.

Tip into the prepared tin. Bake for about 1 hour, or until a skewer, when inserted into the centre comes out clean. Leave to set for a few minutes before turning out on to a wire rack to go cold.

Almond & apricot loaf

4 oz (115 g) dried apricots,
   chopped
2 oz (55 g) butter
5¼ oz (130 g/¾ cup) sugar
1 egg, lightly beaten
4 oz (115 g/1 cup)
   wholemeal (whole-wheat)
   flour
4 oz (115 g/1 cup) plain
   (all-purpose) flour
1 teaspoon baking soda
2 oz (55 g/½ cup) almonds,
   chopped

makes 1 loaf

Preheat the oven to 350°F/180°C/Gas mark 4.
Grease and line a 8 x 6 in (20 x 15 cm) loaf tin (pan).

Combine the apricots, butter, sugar and 8 fl oz
(250 ml/1 cup) boiling water in a bowl. Stir until the
butter melts and the sugar dissolves, then leave to
cool to room temperature.

Stir in egg, then the sifted flours and baking soda in
two batches. Stir in the almonds.

Tip into the prepared baking tin. Bake for 1 hour, or
until golden brown and cooked through. Leave to
set in the tin for a few minutes, before turning out
on to a wire rack to go cold.

Lemon-frosted tea loaf

8 oz (225 g/1 cup) butter,
  softened
2 teaspoons vanilla extract
1 teaspoon finely grated
  lemon zest
14 oz (400 g/2 cups)
  superfine (caster) sugar
6 eggs
6 oz (150 g/1½ cups) plain
  (all-purpose) flour
4 oz (115 g/1 cup)
  self-raising (self-rising)
  flour
8 fl oz (250 ml/1 cup)
  natural (plain) yogurt

FROSTING

6 oz (150 g/1½ cups) icing
  (confectioners') sugar,
  sifted
1 tablespoon lemon juice
1 oz (30 g) butter, softened
2 tablespoons dessicated (dry
  unsweetened shredded)
  coconut, toasted

makes 1 cake

Preheat the oven to 325°F/160°C/Gas mark 3.
Grease and line a 9 in (23 cm) square cake tin (pan).

In a bowl, beat the butter, vanilla and lemon zest
until light and fluffy. Gradually add the sugar, and
beat until creamy. Add the eggs one at a time,
beating well after each addition.

Sift the flours onto the egg and sugar mixture in
batches, alternating with the yogurt and folding in
gently.

Tip into the prepared tin and bake for 1 hour, or
until a skewer comes out clean when inserted
into the centre of the cake. Leave to stand for 10
minutes, then turn out onto a wire rack to go cold.

To make the frosting, mix the icing sugar with the
lemon juice and butter in a bowl until smooth.
Spread over the cake and scatter coconut on top.

tray bakes

Choc-mint brownies

4 oz (115 g/½ cup) butter
7 oz (200 g) dark
    (bittersweet) chocolate,
    broken into pieces
2 eggs
6 oz (175 g/¾ cup) brown
    sugar
2 tablespoons unsweetened
    cocoa powder
4 oz (115 g/1 cup)
    all-purpose (plain) flour
2 tablespoons vegetable oil

TOPPING

4 oz (115 g/1 cup)
    (confectioners') sugar
½ oz (15 g) butter
3 drops peppermint extract

makes 20

Preheat the oven to 325°F/160°C/Gas mark 3.
Grease and line a 9 in (23 cm) square tin (pan).

Melt the butter and chocolate in a medium
saucepan, stir occasionally. Leave to cool slightly.

Beat the eggs and sugar in a large bowl until light
and creamy. Beat in the cocoa, flour and the oil,
then the cooled chocolate mixture.

Pour the batter mixture into the prepared cake tin.
Bake for 40 minutes, or until a skewer inserted into
the centre comes out clean. Turn out onto a wire
rack to go cold.

To make the topping, sift the icing sugar into a
heatproof bowl, add the butter and peppermint
extract, and stir over simmering water until smooth.
Drizzle or pipe the topping over the brownies. Cut
into squares.

Brownies

5 oz (150 g) butter, softened
4 fl oz (120 ml/½ cup)
  honey, warmed
2 eggs, lightly beaten
7 oz (200 g/1¾ cups)
  self-raising (self-rising)
  flour, sifted
5¼ oz (160 g/²/₃ cup brown
  sugar
4 oz (115 g) dark chocolate,
  melted and cooled
icing (confectioners') sugar,
  sifted, for dusting

makes 25

Preheat the oven to 350°F/180°C/Gas mark 4. Grease and line a 9 in (23 cm) square tin (pan).

Put the butter, honey, eggs, flour, brown sugar, melted chocolate and 1 tablespoon of water in a food processor and process until the ingredients are combined.

Tip the batter the prepared cake tin. Bake for 30–35 minutes, or until a skewer, when inserted in the cake centre, comes out clean. Leave to set in the tin for 5 minutes before turning out onto a wire rack to cool completely.

Dust with icing sugar and cut into squares.

Caramel squares

3½ oz (100 g) butter, plus
   extra for greasing
1½ oz (40 g) sugar
3 oz (85 g/¾ cup) cornflour
   (cornstarch), sifted
3 oz (85 g/¾ cup) plain
   (all-purpose) flour, sifted,
   plus extra for dusting

FILLING & TOPPING

4 oz (115 g/½ cup) butter
4 oz (115 g/½ cup) brown
   sugar
2 tablespoons honey
14 oz (400 g) can sweetened
   condensed milk
1 teaspoon vanilla extract
7 oz (200 g) dark
   (semisweet) chocolate,
   melted

makes 24

Preheat the oven to 350°F/180°C/Gas mark 4. Grease and line a 8 x 12in (20 x 30cm) shallow cake tin (pan).

To make the base, beat the butter and sugar in a mixing bowl until light and fluffy. Mix in the cornflour and flour. Turn out onto a lightly floured surface and knead briefly, then press into the prepard tin and bake for 25 minutes or until firm.

To make the filling, put the butter, brown sugar and honey in a saucepan and melt over medium heat, stirring constantly until the sugar dissolves and the ingredients are combined. Bring to the boil and simmer for 7 minutes. Beat in the condensed milk and vanilla extract. Pour the filling over the base and bake for 20 minutes. Set aside to cool completely.

Spread melted chocolate over the filling. Set aside until firm, then cut into squares.

Chocolate rum slices

4 oz (115 g/1 cup)
self-raising (self-rising)
flour, sifted
1 tablespoon unsweetened
cocoa powder, sifted
3½ oz (100 g/½ cup) caster
(superfine) sugar
2½ oz (65 g) desiccated (dry
unsweetened shredded)
coconut, plus extra for
dusting
2½ oz (65 g) raisins, chopped
4 oz (115 g/½ cup) butter,
melted
1 teaspoon rum
2 tablespoons dark
(semisweet) chocolate,
grated (shredded)
2 eggs, lightly beaten

TOPPING
4 oz (115 g/1 cup) icing
(confectioners') sugar
2 tablespoons unsweetened
cocoa powder
½ oz (15 g) butter, softened

makes 25

Preheat the oven to 350°F/180°C/Gas mark 4. Grease and line a 10 in (25 cm) square cake tin (pan).

Put the flour, cocoa powder, sugar, coconut and raisins in a bowl and mix to combine. Stir in the melted butter, rum, grated chocolate and beaten eggs. Mix well to thoroughly combine.

Press the batter into the prepared tin and bake for 20–25 minutes, or until firm. Allow to cool in the tin.

To make the topping, sift the icing sugar and cocoa together into a bowl. Add the butter and 1 tablespoon boiling water, and beat to a spreadable consistency.

Turn the bake out onto a wire rack, spread with topping and dust with extra coconut. Refrigerate until firm, then cut into squares.

Raspberry yogurt slice

3½ oz (100 g) butter
4 oz (115 g/1 cup) plain
  (all-purpose) flour
2 oz (55 g/¼ cup) brown
  sugar
3 oz (80 g/¾ cup) rolled oats

TOPPING
4 oz (115 g) cream cheese
6 fl oz (175 ml/¾ cup)
  raspberry-flavoured
  yogurt
1 tablespoon honey
1 teaspoon lemon juice
1 teaspoon grated lemon zest
1 tablespoon gelatine powder
8 oz (225 g) frozen
  raspberries, thawed
1¾ oz (45 g/¼ cup) sugar

makes about 15

Preheat the oven to 350°F/180°C/Gas mark 4.
Grease and line a deep-sided 11 x 7 in (28 x 18 cm)
baking tray.

Blend the butter and flour together in a food
processor with the sugar until the dough just comes
together. Fold in the oats.

Press into the base of the prepared tray. Bake for
about 15–20 minutes, or until a skewer comes out
clean, then allow to cool.

Beat the cream cheese with the yogurt and honey.
Add the lemon juice and zest.

Scatter the gelatine over 2 fl oz (50 ml/¼ cup) water
to soften.

Heat three-quarters of the raspberries in a pan
and add the sugar and softened gelatine. Bring
to the boil, stirring until the sugar and gelatine
have thoroughly dissolved. Press through a
sieve (strainer), then leave to cool to egg white
consistency. Stir into the cheese and yogurt mixture
with the remaining raspberries.

Pour the yogurt mixture over the base and
refrigerate overnight. Serve with extra raspberries.

Walnut chocolate slice

4 egg whites
1¾ oz (45 g/¼ cup) sugar
4 oz (115 g) chocolate,
   melted and cooled
3 oz (85 g) butter, melted
   and cooled
1½ teaspoons vanilla extract
4 oz (115 g/1 cup) plain
   (all-purpose) flour
2 oz (55 g/¼ cup) brown
   sugar
5 oz (160 g/¹⁄₃ cup)
   unsweetened cocoa powder
2 teaspoons baking powder
½ teaspoon bicarbonate of
   soda (baking soda)
1½ oz (40 g/¹⁄₃ cup) chopped
   walnuts or pecans

makes 25

Preheat the oven to 375°F/190°C/Gas mark 5.
Grease and line a 9 in (23 cm) deep-sided square tin
(pan).

Whisk the egg whites in a clearn grease-free bowl
until soft peaks form. Gradually beat in the sugar.
and continue until it dissolves. Fold in the melted
chocolate and butter and the vanilla extract.

Into a large bowl sift the flour, brown sugar, cocoa,
baking powder and bicarbonate of soda. Make
a well in the centre. Fold in the egg whites and
walnuts until just combined. Tip into the prepared
tin and smooth out to the corners.

Bake for 20–25 minutes, or until cooked when tested
with a skewer. Cool in the pan. Cut into 1½–2 in
(4–5 cm) squares.

Marzipan triangles

3½ oz (100 g/1 cup) rolled oats

3½ oz (100 g/½ cup) caster (superfine) sugar

4 oz (115 g/1 cup) self-raising (self-rising) flour, sifted

3 oz (85 g/¾ cup) ground almonds (almond meal)

1 tablespoon golden (light corn) syrup

4 fl oz (120 ml/½ cup) canola oil

1 egg

¼ teaspoon almond extract

8 oz (225 g) marzipan (almond paste)

1 ½ oz (40 g/⅓ cup flaked (sliced) almonds, to decorate

makes 42

Preheat oven to 350°F/180°C/Gas mark 4. Grease and line a deep-sided 12 x 8 in (30 x 20 cm) baking tray.

Combine the oats, sugar, flour and ground almonds in a bowl. Stir in the golden syrup, oil, egg and almond extract.

Spread half the mixture evenly over base of the prepared tray.

Roll out the marzipan to fit the tray and cover the oats mixture. Top with the remaining batter. Scatter flaked almonds on top. Press into the mixture.

Bake for 30 minutes, or until golden. Leave to set for 10 minutes, then turn out on to a wire rack to go cold. Cut into triangles.

Pumpkin nut slice

6 oz (175 g/¾ cup) butter

7 oz (200 g/1 cup) caster (superfine) sugar

4 oz (115 g/1 cup) plain (all-purpose) flour

1 ½ teaspoon baking powder

1½ teaspoons ground cinnamon powder

½ teaspoon mixed (apple pie) spice

2 eggs, lightly beaten

2 oz (55 g/½ cup) chopped pecans or walnuts

½ teaspoon vanilla extract

3 oz (85 g/½ cup) chopped raisins

5½ oz (165 g/1 cup) drained, crushed pineapple

4 oz (115 g/¾ cup) cooked, mashed pumpkin

TOPPING

6 oz (150 g/1½ cups) icing (confectioners') sugar

8 oz (225 g) cream cheese, softened

½ teaspoon vanilla extract

2 teaspoons lemon juice

makes 6–8

Preheat the oven to 350°F/180°C/Gas mark 4. Grease and line a 9 in (23 cm) square tin (pan).

Beat the butter and sugar in a large bowl until light and fluffy.

Sift the flour, baking powder and spices over and stir to blend. Beat in the beaten eggs.

Stir in the nuts, vanilla extract, raisins, pineapple and pumpkin. Mix well and pour into the prepared tin.

Bake for 1 hour, or until a skewer inserted in the centre of the cake comes out clean. Leave to set for a few minutes before turning out on to a wire rack to go cold.

To·make the icing, place all the ingredients in a mixing bowl and beat until well combined, then increase speed and beat until light and fluffy. Spread icing over the cake.

Carrot & almond squares

4 oz (115 g/1 cup)
  wholemeal (whole-wheat)
  self-raising (self-rising)
  flour
1 oz (30 g/¼ cup)
  wheatgerm
1 teaspoon bicarbonate of
  soda (baking soda)
1 teaspoon ground cinnamon
  powder
1 teaspoon ground nutmeg
4 fl oz (120 ml/½ cup)
  vegetable oil
5½ oz (160 g/⅓ cup) honey
3 eggs, lightly beaten
7 oz (200 g) grated
  (shredded) carrot, lightly
  packed
2 oz (55 g/½ cup) chopped
  walnuts
3 oz (85 g/½ cup) well
  drained, crushed pineapple
almonds, to decorate
glacé cherries, to decorate

makes about 15

Preheat the oven to 350°F/180°C/Gas mark 4.
Grease and line a deep-sided 11 x 7 in (28 x 18 cm)
baking tray.

Sift the flour, wheatgerm, bicarbonate of soda,
cinnamon and nutmeg in a bowl.

Beat the oil, honey and eggs together in another
bowl until well combined, then pour into the dry
ingredients and beat until smooth.

Stir in the grated carrot, walnuts and pineapple and
mix well.

Tip into the prepared tin, smoothing the top level.
Decorate the top with almonds and glacé cherries.

Bake for 35–40 minutes, or until golden brown.
Leave to cool in the tin for 5 minutes, then turn out
onto a wire rack to cool. Cut into squares.

pies & tarts

Individual meat pies

1 lb 11 oz (750 g) shortcrust
   pastry
13 oz (375 g) puff pastry
1 egg, lightly beaten

FILLING
1 lb 11 oz (750 g) lean
   minced (ground) beef
16 fl oz (475 ml/2 cups) beef
   stock
freshly ground black pepper
2 tablespoons cornflour
   (cornstarch), blended with
   4 fl oz (120 ml/½ cup)
   water
1 tablespoon Worcestershire
   sauce
1 teaspoon soy sauce

makes 8

Preheat the oven to 425°F/220°C/Gas mark 7.

To make the filling, heat a frying pan over a medium heat, add the meat and cook until brown. Drain off the juices, stir in the stock, season with black pepper, to taste, and bring to the boil. Reduce the heat, cover and simmer for 20 minutes.

Stir in the cornflour mixture, Worcestershire and soy sauces and cook, stirring, until the mixture boils and thickens. Cool.

Roll out the shortcrust pastry to ¼ in (5 mm) thick and use to line the base and sides of eight buttered, small metal pie dishes.

Roll out the puff pastry to ¼ in (5 mm) thick and cut out rounds to fit the top of the pies.

Divide the filling between the pie dishes. Brush the edges of the shortcrust pastry with water, top with rounds of puff pastry and press the edges together to seal. Brush the pies with egg and bake for 5 minutes, then reduce the oven temperature to 350°F/180°C/Gas mark 4 and bake for another 10–15 minutes, or until pastry is golden.

Cornish pasties

2 oz (55 g/¼ cup) butter,
    chilled, plus extra for
    greasing
2 oz (55 g/¼ cup) lard or
    white vegetable fat chilled
8 oz (225 g/2 cups) plain
    (all-purpose) flour, sifted,
    plus extra for dusting
1 egg, lightly beaten

FILLING

8 oz (225 g lean minced
    (ground) beef
1 small onion, grated
    (shredded)
1 potato, peeled and grated
    (shredded)
½ small turnip, peeled and
    grated (shredded)
¼ cup fresh parsley, chopped
1 tablespoon Worcestershire
    sauce
freshly ground black pepper

makes 6

Preheat the oven to 425°F/220°C/Gas mark 7.
Lightly grease a baking sheet.

To make the pastry, cut the butter and lard into the
flour in a large bowl and rub in, using your fingertips,
until the mixture resembles breadcrumbs. Mix in
enough cold water (about 2½ fl oz /75 ml/¹/₃ cup) to
form a soft dough, then turn the pastry out onto a
floured surface and knead lightly. Wrap in cling film
(plastic wrap) and chill for 30 minutes.

Meanwhile, combine all the filling ingredients in a
bowl and mix well.

Roll out the pastry on a lightly floured surface to
¼ in (6 mm) thick and, using an upturned saucer
as a guide, cut out six 6 in (15 cm) rounds. Divide
the filling between the pastry rounds. Brush the
edges with water and fold the pastry rounds in
half enclosing the filling. Press the pastry edges
together fluting them between your finger and
thumb to seal.

Place on the prepared baking sheet, brush with
egg and bake for 15 minutes. Reduce the oven
temperature to 325°F/160°C/Gas mark 3 and bake
for 20 minutes more, or until golden.

Leek & dill tart

10 oz (275 g) shortcrust
  pastry

FILLING

1 tablespoon butter
4 leeks, trimmed and thinly
  sliced
8 fl oz (250 ml/1 cup)
  natural (plain) yogurt
1 tablespoon plain
  (all-purpose) flour
2 eggs, lightly beaten
3 oz (85 g) Cheddar cheese,
  grated (shredded)
½ bunch fresh dill, chopped
freshly ground black pepper

serves 4

Preheat the oven to 400°F/200°C/Gas mark 6. Roll out the pastry to line a lightly greased 8 in (20 cm) loose-base tart pan. Prick the base several times with a fork, line with baking paper and half-fill with baking beans. Bake for 8–10 minutes, remove the beans and paper and bake for another 5 minutes, until pastry is golden. Set aside to cool.

To make the filling, melt the butter in a frying pan and cook the leeks for 4–5 minutes, or until just tender.

Place the yogurt, flour, eggs, three-quarters of the cheese and 1 tablespoon of dill in a bowl and mix to combine. Fold in the leeks, season to taste with black pepper and spoon into the pastry case.

Sprinkle the tart with the remaining cheese and dill and bake for 20 minutes, or until tart is set.

Potato, egg & leek pies

1 lb (450 g) shortcrust
 pastry

FILLING

1 oz (30 g) butter
4 leeks, sliced
2 cloves garlic, crushed
2 teaspoons curry powder
6 potatoes, cooked until
 tender and diced
10½ oz (290 g) asparagus,
 stalks removed, blanched
 and chopped
4 hard boiled eggs, diced
4 oz (115 g) mature Cheddar
 cheese, grated (shredded)
¼ cup fresh parsley, chopped
¼ pint (150 ml/⅔ cup sour
 cream
1 egg and 2 yolks, lightly
 beaten, plus 1 egg for
 glazing
freshly ground black pepper
1 tablespoon caraway seeds

makes 10

Preheat the oven to 425°F/220°C/Gas mark 7.

To make the filling, melt the butter in a frying pan over a low heat, add the leeks and cook for 3–4 minutes, or until soft. Increase the heat to medium, stir in the garlic and curry powder and cook for 1 minute.

In a bowl, combine the potatoes, leek mixture, asparagus, eggs, cheese, parsley, sour cream and black pepper, to taste. Set aside.

Meanwhile roll out the shortcrust to ⅕ in (5 mm) thick, and cut to fit the base and sides of ten buttered, metal pie dishes. Cut the remaining pastry to fit the top of the pies.

Spoon the filling into the pie dishes, brush the pastry edges with beaten egg and top with pie lids. Press the pastry edges together, to seal. Using a sharp knife, make a slit on the top of each pie, then brush with beaten egg and dust with caraway seeds.

Bake for 15 minutes. Reduce the oven temperature to 350°F/180°C/Gas mark 4 and bake for 15 minutes, or until golden.

Leek & apple pie

13 oz (370 g) shortcrust
  pastry

LEEK FILLING
1 tablespoon butter
1 cooking apple, cored, peeled
  and sliced
3 small leeks, sliced
4 rashers (strips) bacon,
  chopped
¼ teaspoon ground cloves
¼ teaspoon ground nutmeg
2 oz (55 g) blue cheese,
  crumbled
3 eggs, lightly beaten
6 fl oz (175 ml/¾ cup)
  double (heavy) cream
2 tablespoons port (optional)
freshly ground black pepper

makes 1 pie

Preheat the oven to 425°F/220°C/Gas mark 7.

To make the filling, melt the butter in a frying
pan and cook the apple, leeks and bacon over a
medium heat for 5–8 minutes, or until apple softens.
Add the cloves and nutmeg and cook for 1 minute
longer. Set aside to cool.

Roll out the pastry on a lightly floured surface and
line the base and sides of a lightly greased 9 in
(23 cm) flan tin (pan). Prick the base of the pastry
with a fork, line with baking paper and half-fill with
baking beans. Bake for 10 minutes. Remove the
beans and paper. Reduce the oven temperature to
350°F/180°C/Gas mark 4.

Spread the apple mixture over the base of the
pastry case.

In a bowl, mix the cheese, eggs, cream, port (if
using) and black pepper, to taste, to combine and
carefully pour into the pastry case. Bake for
30–35 minutes, or until pie is firm.

Traditional lemon chiffon pie

8 oz (225 g) oatmeal biscuits
  (cookies)
2½ oz (65 g) butter

LEMON FILLING
4 eggs, separated
5¼ oz (130 g/¾ cup) caster
  (superfine) sugar
zest of 1 lemon, finely grated
  (shredded)
juice of 2 lemons
2 teaspoons gelatine powder
2 fl oz (50 ml/¼ cup) white
  wine

makes 1 pie

Put the oatmeal biscuits in batches by placing them in a sealed plastic bag and crush by rolling over with a rolling pin, or crush in the bowl of a food processor. Melt the butter in a small pan, then tip into the crushed biscuits and mix to combine.

Press the mixture into a lightly greased 9 in (23 cm) springform tin, pressing the crumbs up the sides. Chill the case until ready to fill.

To make the filling, put egg yolks, 2 oz (55 g/½ cup) sugar and the lemon zest in a mixing bowl and beat until light and fluffy.

Pour the lemon juice into a small saucepan and bring to the boil. Pour into the egg yolk mixture in a steady stream, while beating constantly.

Put the gelatine and wine in a small bowl and set over a saucepan of simmering water until dissolved. Stir the gelatine mixture into the egg yolk mixture.

Beat the egg whites in a grease-free bowl and beat until stiff peaks form. Add the remaining sugar and beat for 3 minutes longer. Fold into the egg yolk mixture, then spoon the filling into biscuit crumb case. Refrigerate for 2–3 hour, or until set.

Spicy pumpkin pie

4 oz (115 g/1 cup) plain
  (all-purpose) flour, plus
  extra for dusting
½ teaspoon baking powder
3½ oz (100 g) butter, chilled
  and diced, plus extra for
  greasing
1½ tablespoon caster
  (superfine) sugar
1 egg yolk, lightly beaten

FILLING

10 oz (275 g) pumpkin purée
2 eggs, lightly beaten
4 fl oz (120 ml/½ cup) sour
  cream
4 fl oz (120 ml/½ cup)
  double (heavy) cream
3 oz (86 g/¼ cup) golden
  (light corn) syrup
½ teaspoon ground nutmeg
½ teaspoon ground mixed
  (apple pie) spice
½ teaspoon ground cinnamon
whipped cream, to serve

makes 1 pie

Preheat the oven to 400°F/200°C/Gas mark 6.

To make the pastry, sift the flour and baking powder into a mixing bowl. Rub in the butter with cold fingertips until the mixture resembles coarse breadcrumbs, then stir in the sugar. Make a well in the centre and mix in the egg and a drizzle of cold water and mix to a firm dough. Turn out onto a floured surface and knead lightly until smooth. Wrap in cling film (plastic) wrap and chill for 30 minutes.

To make the filling, place the pumpkin purée, eggs, sour cream, cream, golden syrup, nutmeg, mixed spice and cinnamon in a mixing bowl and beat until smooth and well combined.

Roll out the pastry and use to line a greased 9 in (23 cm) flan tin with removable base.

Spoon the filling into the pastry case. Bake for 20 minutes, then reduce the heat to 320°F/160°/Gas mark 3 and bake for 25–30 minutes longer, or until the filling is set and the pastry golden. Allow to set in the tin for 5 minutes before removing. Serve hot, warm or cold with whipped cream.

Rhubarb & apple tart

4 oz (115 g/1 cup) plain
  (all-purpose) flour, sifted,
  plus extra for dusting
2 teaspoons icing sugar,
  sifted
3 oz (85 g) butter, chilled and
  diced, plus extra for
  greasing

FILLING

6 stalks rhubarb, chopped
3 oz (90 g) sugar
1 oz (30 g) butter
3 cooking apples, cored,
  peeled and sliced
4 oz (115 g) cream cheese
1 teaspoon vanilla extract
1 egg

makes 1 tart

To make the pastry, put the flour and icing sugar in a large bowl and rub in the butter, using your fingertips, until the mixture resembles coarse breadcrumbs. Add 4 teaspoons iced water and knead to a smooth dough. Wrap in cling film (plastic wrap) and refrigerate for 30 minutes.

Preheat the oven to 400°F/200°C/Gas mark 6. Roll out the pastry on a lightly floured surface and use to line a buttered 9 in (23 cm) fluted flan tin. Line the pastry case with baking paper and baking beans. Bake for 15 minutes. Remove the beans and paper and cook for 5 minutes longer. Reduce the oven temperature to 350°F/180°C/Gas mark 4.

To make the filling, poach the rhubarb until tender. Drain then stir in 2 tablespoons of the sugar and set aside to cool.

Melt the butter in a frying pan and cook the apples for 3–4 minutes. Set aside to cool.

Place cream cheese, rest of the sugar, vanilla and egg in a bowl and beat until smooth. Spoon the rhubarb into pastry case, top with cream cheese mixture and arrange the apple slices on top. Bake for 40–45 minutes, or until filling is firm.

Apple chiffon tart

13 oz (370 g) shortcrust
   pastry

FILLING & TOPPING
4 teaspoons gelatine powder
2 large cooking apples,
   peeled, cored and diced
2 egg whites
1 tablespoon caster
   (superfine) sugar
8 fl oz (250 ml/1 cup) double
   (heavy) cream
1½ oz (40 g/½ cup)
   dessicated (dry
   unsweetened shredded)
   coconut
2 oz (55 g/¼ cup) brown
   sugar

makes 1 tart

Preheat the oven to 400°F/200°C/Gas mark 6.

Roll out the pastry on a lightly floured surface and use to line a buttered 9 in (23 cm) fluted flan tin. Line the pastry case with baking paper and baking beans. Bake for 15 minutes. Remove the beans and paper and cook for 5 minutes longer. Leave to cool.

Put the apples in a small pan with a drizzle of water and cook over medium heat until soft and puréed. Leave to go cold. Set aside quarter of the purée.

Add the gelatine to 2 fl oz 50 ml (¼ cup) hot water and stir briskly with a fork until dissolved. Stir in to the large quantity of apple purée.

In a bowl, whisk the egg whites until stiff. Gradually whisk in the sugar. Fold in half the cream then tip into the apple mixture. Mix to combine. Pour into the pastry case. Chill until set.

Spread the remaining apple purée over the top of the tart. Scatter the coconut and brown sugar on top. Whip the remaining cream and pipe around the edge.

Strawberry tarts

4 oz (115 g/½ cup) butter
2 oz (55 g) sugar
1 egg
2 teaspoons milk
8 oz (225 g) self-raising
    (self-rising) flour, sifted,
    plus extra for dusting
6 oz (175 g) strawberry jam
    (jelly)

TOPPING
2 oz (55 g) sugar
2 oz (55 g) desiccated (dry
    unsweetened shredded)
    coconut
1 egg

makes 24

Preheat the oven to 400°F/200°C/Gas mark 6.
Lightly grease two or three bun tins (patty pans)

Put the butter and sugar in a mixing bowl and beat
until light and fluffy. Mix in the egg and milk, then
add the flour, mixing to form a dough. Turn out onto
a lightly floured surface and roll out to ¼ in
(4 mm) thick. Stamp out rounds using a 3 in (7.5 cm)
cookie cutter and place the prepared bun tins. Top
each with a spoonful of jam.

To make the topping, place sugar, coconut and egg
in a bowl and mix well. Place a spoonful of topping
on each tart and bake for 10–15 minutes, or until the
tops are golden and bases are cooked.

Orange chocolate tarts

13 oz (370 g) shortcrust
  pastry
flour, for dusting
4 oz (115 g) dark
  (bittersweet) chocolate,
  melted

FILLING

3 egg yolks
2 tablespoons sugar
½ pint (300 ml/1¼ cups)
  milk, scalded
zest of ½ orange, finely
  grated
2 tablespoons Grand
  Marnier (orange liqueur)
1½ teaspoons gelatine
  powder, dissolved in 4
  teaspoons hot water,
  cooled
2 fl oz (50 ml/¼ cup) double
  (heavy) cream, whipped

makes 6

Preheat the oven to 400°F/200°C/Gas mark 6.

Roll out the pastry on a lightly floured surface to a thickness of ¼ in (4 mm) and use to line six 4 in (10 cm) flan tins. Line the pastry cases with baking paper and half-fill with baking beans.

Bake for 8 minutes, then remove the beans and paper and bake for 10 minutes longer, or until the pastry is golden. Set aside to cool completely. Brush the cold pastry cases with melted chocolate and set aside until the chocolate sets.

To make the filling, put the egg yolks and sugar in a heatproof mixing bowl and set over a saucepan of simmering water. Beat until a ribbon trail forms when the beater is lifted from the mixture. Remove the bowl from the heat and gradually whisk in the milk. Transfer the mixture to a heavy pan and cook over low heat, stirring in a figure-of-eight pattern, until the mixture thickens and coats the back of a wooden spoon. Do not allow the mixture to boil. Remove from the heat, place in a bowl of ice cold water and stir until cool.

Stir in the remaining ingredients, then spoon the filling into the pastry cases. Chill until set.

Index

Published in 2014 by
New Holland Publishers
London • Sydney • Cape Town • Auckland

The Chandlery Unit 114 50 Westminster Bridge Road London SE1 7QY UK
1/66 Gibbes Street Chatswood NSW 2067 Australia
Wembley Square First Floor Solan Road Gardens Cape Town 8001 South Africa
218 Lake Road Northcote Auckland New Zealand

www.newhollandpublishers.com

A catalogue record of this book is available at the British Library and the
National Library of Australia.

ISBN: 9781742574837

Publisher: Fiona Schultz
Design: Lorena Susak
Production Director: Olga Dementiev

Texture: Shutterstock

Printer: Toppan Leefung Printing Ltd (China)

10 9 8 7 6 5 4 3 2 1

Follow New Holland Publishers on
Facebook: www.facebook.com/NewHollandPublishers